# Images from the Inside Passage

*An Alaskan Portrait by Winter & Pond*

This early view of Juneau shows the town in the foreground. Douglas and Treadwell are across Gastineau Channel, on Douglas Island. Winter and Pond may have obtained the negative from an earlier photographer, for the date 1889 is inscribed on the glass plate.

# Images from the Inside Passage

## An Alaskan Portrait by Winter & Pond

VICTORIA WYATT

University of Washington Press, *Seattle and London*, in association with the Alaska State Library, *Juneau*

This book is published in connection with the exhibit IMAGES FROM THE INSIDE PASSAGE: AN ALASKAN PORTRAIT BY WINTER & POND, based on the Winter and Pond Collection at the Alaska State Library. The exhibition and publication were supported by a grant from the National Endowment for the Humanities.

Division of State Libraries
Department of Education, State of Alaska
William G. Demmert, Commissioner; Karen R. Crane, Director

Designed by Audrey Meyer
Composition by the Department of Printing, University of Washington
Printed and bound by Toppan Printing, Tokyo

The Winter and Pond photographs used in this volume were prepared by Ronald E. Klein from the original glass plate and nitrate negatives.

Library of Congress Cataloging-in-Publication Data

Wyatt, Victoria.
    Images from the inside passage : an Alaskan portrait by Winter and Pond / Victoria Wyatt.
        p.    cm.
Bibliography: p.
Includes index.
ISBN 0-295-96812-5 (cl.)
ISBN 0-295-96835-4 (pbk.)
    1. Tlingit Indians—Pictorial works. 2. Haida Indians—Pictorial works. 3. Indians of North America—Alaska—Pictorial works. 4. Winter, Lloyd. 5. Pond, E. Percy. I. Title.
E99.T6W93  1989
979.8'00497—dc19                    88-34376

*A young Lloyd Winter poses in the studio, dressed as a hunter with beaded boots, hatband, and, possibly, Eskimo mukluks.*

# Contents

*Around the turn of the century, as their business
expanded, Winter and Pond moved to the Horseshoe
Building on Front and Main, where they stayed until
1918.*

# Foreword

WE ALL RECOGNIZE THE OLD SAW COMPARING THE RELATIVE value of photograph and words as testimony to the story-telling capacity of photographic images. A single photograph is capable of evoking several thousand words, for its story is not a singular one. The scene, the characters, are set pieces from which each viewer scripts a version of the story, based upon personal experience, knowledge, values, and other cultural baggage. Photographs from the past and from other cultures are particularly evocative and challenging, for there are more unknowns and more detective work involved in the unfolding of their stories. The images from the collection of Juneau photographers Winter and Pond exhibited in *Images from the Inside Passage* offer a wealth of stories which speak to many audiences.

For the author/curator of this publication and exhibit, historian Victoria Wyatt, the images tell most strongly of the changes wrought in Indians' lives in the more than one hundred years following contact and sub-sequent settlement of southeastern Alaska: the wearing of European clothing and its combination with Native dance regalia; the introduction of European-style houses; the architectural innovations made to tradi-tional plank houses; the curio trade in Native objects coexistent with the still important ceremonial role of Native art; changing practices and alterations in mortuary art. Wyatt draws attention to the success of these photographers in presenting the range and complexity of Indian life in southeastern Alaska at the turn of the century, but cautions that there is no typical view. The story of contact and change as told through the Winter and Pond images is noteworthy for rendering the legacy of south-eastern Alaska and its people visible and tangible. As Wyatt suggests, through the images the people and their experiences become real.

For me, as an anthropologist, it is the many unfinished stories in the images that hold the highest interest. The beaded ceremonial costumes speak of ancient trade relationships with Athabaskans of the interior and Native admiration for foreign military uniforms; the ceremonial regalia photographed and displayed first in one house and then in another and the costumes that have been dismantled and donned by two separate individuals invite thought about the changing relationship between the people and their ceremonial art. The numerous items displayed in photographs of the Whale House and Raven House at Klukwan urge one to follow their subsequent histories to learn more of early collecting activities at Klukwan and the art which remained in Native hands.

The image of Indian art as Winter and Pond arranged it in their curio shop also begs telling. Their display of goods, carefully recorded by their camera, resembles that of other curio shops of the time in its dark Victorian clutter. But did the pieces come to them from Native artisans off the streets in Juneau, and/or were their photo expeditions combined with collecting expeditions? And what of their aesthetics in collecting Native art?

Winter and Pond's portraits of Alaskan Indians, though anonymous and informationally poorer than the images of villages and ceremonies, nonetheless have their stories. My favorite is the Tlingit woman (no. 16), drawn up to her full height, silver braceleted arms akimbo, staring seriously if not haughtily at the camera. She wears a hat, an elegant beaded and fringed bodice, and her finest long ruffled dress to which a small nautically attired boy (her son?) clings; a Chilkat dancing blanket tacked to the photographer's backdrop is a reminder of who they are.

Buried within the images is also a story of contact between photographer and subject. Winter and Pond's currency among these Native people is evident in the kinds of photographic work they produced. They visit a family's fish camp, have access to the three most important houses at Klukwan, attend potlatches (or at least the potlatch preliminaries), and are allowed or commissioned to photograph the dead lying in state. Despite Winter and Pond's employment of certain photographic conventions that appear contrived to us today, the Native people who posed for their camera seem genuine, as does the photographers' respect for them. These are not typical "Studio Indians."

And what stories did the photographs tell to their contemporaries? Which images caught the eye of the tourist sorting through the pile of postcards in Winter and Pond's curio shop? Did the members of the Whale House at Klukwan own a copy of the much circulated photograph of their ceremonial house and its clan art or was this image only of interest to tourists preserving memories of their Alaska trip? And did Winter and Pond's Native customers use the images of themselves in the same ways that their non-Native portrait sitters did?

Viewers of the photographs today will have their own stories to tell. Native people may be able to add to our current ethnographic and historical understanding of the photographs, museum curators or art specialists may identify the whereabouts and the history of the art pieces depicted. Other researchers may be prompted to pick up the threads of stories begun—to compare, say, Winter and Pond's portraiture of Native people with the large body of portraits of non-Natives that survive in their collection, or to relate Winter and Pond's views of Tlingit people to those of contemporary image-makers Vincent Soboleff, E. W. Merrill, W. H. Case, and Herbert Draper. As Wyatt notes, the images raise—and will continue to raise—many more questions than they answer. To me, the greatest intrigue of historical photographs is in the very curiosity they arouse, in the stories begun but never really ended.

*Margaret B. Blackman, Brockport, New York*

*Tlingit dancers display ceremonial art in the
Whale House of the village of Klukwan in 1895.
Winter and Pond produced this image as a
postcard, as the masking indicates.*

# Preface

THE INDIANS OF THE PACIFIC NORTHWEST COAST HAVE A tradition of spectacular art in company with dramatic songs, dances, and myths. Up and down the Northwest Coast, Indians created a culture of images and imagery. Tlingit and Haida Indians of southeast Alaska—the primary subjects of the photographs featured here—contributed with other coastal groups to artistic achievements found nowhere else on earth.[1]

Contact with foreign settlers produced rapid changes in Native Alaskan culture. Missionaries brought new religions and new education systems. Caucasian civil authorities introduced a new legal code. Businessmen established canneries and mines, often appropriating the fishing and hunting lands on which Indians relied for subsistence. Many Caucasians opposed Native cultural expression and fought to suppress it.

The presence of the foreigners in Alaska touched every aspect of Native life. Some of the changes they brought were welcomed by Indians; many more were forced. Indians met the traumatic transitions with strength, pragmatism, and a determination to survive as a people. They faced painful choices. The cultural revival among their descendants today attests to their judgment.

Historical photographs are tremendous resources for documenting changes Indians experienced. Since Indians in southeast Alaska did not often leave written records before the turn of the century, most written historical sources reflect the point of view of someone foreign to their culture. Like these written records, photographs are also from an outsider's vantage point, but they cannot avoid showing many aspects of Native experience, thereby supplementing written records. Just as important, in photographs the people can shine through in all their expressive humanity. No longer abstractions, they come to life. Written words may quickly fade from memory; images endure.

A picture may well be worth a thousand words, but as historical documents, photographs are subject to the same questions as written documents. Despite initial appearances, photographs are not objective.[2] Photographic images were created for specific purposes and for certain audiences. No photograph can be accepted as "representative" of a way of life without additional documentation. The many factors that influenced what photographs show include the wishes and capabilities of the photographers, and the responses of the Indians.[3] At the turn of the century, it was necessary for photographers to carry cumbersome equipment, to have sufficient light, and to choose motionless subjects.

Recognizing subjective variables, and how they influence perspective, is frequently more difficult in images than in written sources. This does not make photographs less valuable as resources; the form of the evidence they provide is simply somewhat different. Often photographs are indispensable to historical research not because of the answers they provide, but because of the questions they inspire.

Many aspects of human experience are matters of attitudes and of values, not of facts. These matters cannot be scientifically quantified, tested, or verified, but if they are ignored in research, some of the most fundamental elements of human life go unstudied. What good is it to know what happened, if we do not ask what it meant to the people affected?

Photographs provide useful insights into experiences, attitudes, and values. Winter and Pond's images are much more than a record of what people wore or did. They remind us to think about hopes, commitments, and loves—about the intangible spiritual and emotional realms that are the essence of a person. They raise vital questions about sentiments toward culture and ethnic identity, and suggest how Indians cared about their art in the midst of rapid economic, political, and religious change. Certainly the photographs evoke questions concerning the ways Indians and whites perceived each other. Several of the images suggest that Indians did not always pose passively, entirely manipulated by the photographers (see, for example, nos. 66 and 70). Sometimes they took an active role in defining the content or atmosphere of a photograph, and had their own motivations for doing so.

1. See Wilson Duff, "Report of the British Columbia Provincial Museum for 1957," as quoted in Marjorie M. Halpin, *Totem Poles: An Illustrated Guide* (Vancouver: University of British Columbia Press; Seattle: University of Washington Press, 1981), p. 15.

2. For discussions of potentially misleading components of historical photographs, see Joanna Scherer, "Pictures as Documents: Resources for the Study of North American Ethnohistory," and "You Can't Believe Your Eyes: Inaccuracies in Photographs of North American Indians," *Studies in the Anthropology of Visual Communications*, vol. 2, no. 2 (Fall 1975), pp. 65–79; and Ronald Weber, "Photographs as Ethnographic Documents," *Arctic Anthropology*, vol. 22, no. 1 (1985), pp. 67–78.

3. Margaret B. Blackman discusses responses of Indians to photographers in " 'Copying People': Northwest Coast Native Responses to Early Photography," *B.C. Studies*, no. 52 (1981–82), pp. 86–108.

Northwest Coast Indians have strong cultures—cultures that have equipped them to adapt to major changes forced on them by foreigners and by circumstance. The Winter and Pond photographs document those changes in southeast Alaska, and show individual and collective responses to them. Several of the photographs, such as those depicting changes in architecture and in grave sites (for example, nos. 48, 49, 60), show some movement away from time-honored forms of cultural expression. However, these images are in no way a record of a dying culture. They are a reflection of a culture helping its people to keep on living.

The photographs in this publication provide an historical illustration of the impact of foreign contact on Native peoples. They bear witness to the state of Indian-white relations, indicate patterns of adaptation, and suggest much about cultural pride and ethnic identity. They are also a rich source of ethnographic information, affording vivid views of masterpieces of art and enduring forms of cultural expression. My objective here is to discuss the images in various contexts, while laying primary emphasis on historical interpretation.

*Percy Pond stands on the dock in Juneau.*

# Acknowledgments

THIS PUBLICATION AND THE EXHIBITION IT DOCUMENTS OWE their existence to the aid of innumerable supportive individuals and institutions. The National Endowment for the Humanities provided generous funding for the project throughout its planning and implementation, and their staff were always ready with helpful information. The Alaska State Library and the Alaska Department of Education sponsored the project, providing invaluable staff support, administration, equipment, and cost sharing. The University of Washington kindly permitted me leave to devote time to Winter and Pond work.

The project was conceived by William Jorgenson of Juneau, Alaska, who donated an extensive collection of original glass plate and nitrate negatives by Lloyd Winter and Percy Pond to the Alaska State Library in 1981. A personal friend of the photographers, he recognized the vital importance of the images and wanted to make it possible for them to be circulated widely in a traveling exhibition. The Alaska State Legislature provided funds to make prints and copy negatives from the original negatives.

Richard Engen, former director of the Alaska State Library, offered the sponsorship of the Alaska State Library and helped instrumentally during the planning stage. Karen Crane, present director, shared this commitment and gave wholehearted support and valuable assistance during the implementation stage. Norman Johnson of the Alaska State Library administered the grant with efficient good humor. Phyllis DeMuth, Verda Carey, and other library staff at the Alaska State Library were always ready with cheerful assistance.

Ron Klein, technical director of the project, printed the images from the original glass plate and nitrate negatives for display in the exhibition and for reproduction in this book. An accomplished photographer, he brought to this project an extensive expertise in historical photography. In his dedication to pay full tribute to Winter and Pond's excellence, he also vividly demonstrated his own. In addition, he worked with me closely in developing themes and selecting images for inclusion in the exhibition and publication.

Numerous individuals gave indispensable commentary about the content of the photographs. I am especially grateful for the contributions of the many individuals—elders, artists, and scholars—who gave insights about the images and suggested other people to consult; there are additional words in Appendix A about the vital nature of their assistance.

Margaret Blackman read early and late drafts of the publication text very carefully and helped with the project in many other important ways. I am grateful to her for writing the Foreword. Robert De Armond, who has lent valuable insights and support from the beginning of the project, continued to do so in reading the publication draft. I am also indebted to Bill Holm, who was characteristically generous in sharing his time and expertise in commenting on the draft. Conversations with Steve Brown, Bruce Cato, Peter Corey, Nora Dauenhauer, Dale De Armond, Alison Fujino, Roberta Haines, Ellen Hope Hayes, Ira Jacknis, Anna Katzeek, Pat and Frank Roppel, Martha Sandweiss, and many, many others have helped greatly in several aspects of the exhibition and book. Claire Winter, Lloyd Winter's niece, graciously shared with me some original Winter and Pond photographs.

I thank Naomi Pascal and the editorial staff at University of Washington Press for enthusiastically embracing the publication. The book has benefitted from the thoughtful editing of Marilyn Trueblood, who made those stages of production truly enjoyable. Audrey Meyers' respectful design makes every plate a featured photograph. Margaret Davidson created the map of southeast Alaska which appears in this publication and in the exhibition.

I thank the Alaska State Museum for hosting the exhibition during its opening, and the many other institutions in North America that will host it as it travels. I appreciate the support and input from my colleagues at the School of Art and the Thomas Burke Memorial Washington State Museum, both at the University of Washington. I am grateful to Jim Stey and David and Rose Mary Bush, all of Juneau, for supporting the research with their hospitality during my visits to Juneau. I also thank my parents Laurence and Muriel Wyatt and my brother Geoffrey Wyatt for many thoughtful favors during the project.

It is always a pleasure to begin writing acknowledgments, and always a frustration to have to end. It never seems possible to thank individually all the many people who helped, or to pay full tribute to their far-reaching contributions. The work is much the better for all their kindnesses and insights; any errors are my own.

This publication is dedicated to the Tlingit and Haida people who, in these images, speak to us from the past; and to their descendants, who celebrate their rich legacy today.

*This is the original site of Winter and Pond's studio, at*
*222 Front Street.*

# Introduction

LLOYD WINTER AND E. PERCY POND OPERATED THEIR COMMERCIAL photography studio in Juneau, Alaska, from 1893 to 1943. Before moving to Alaska, Winter had studied at the California School of Design in San Francisco and painted portraits. Pond, six years Winter's junior, had been a clerk and bookkeeper in San Francisco. The two met there at the YMCA, where Winter taught swimming. Sharing an interest in athletics, they became good friends.[1]

Both men were intrigued by the potential riches offered by gold mining. In March of 1893, at age twenty-seven, Winter traveled to Juneau to explore mining possibilities. He immediately found a promising opportunity of a different nature. George M. Landerking, a former machinist's mate in the Navy who had established a photography studio in Juneau two years before, invited the painter to join him as a partner.[2] In accepting, Winter became one of a handful of professional photographers in Alaska.[3]

The firm of Landerking and Winter operated until July, when Winter purchased the business from Landerking.[4] Pond, recently arrived from San Francisco, became Winter's new partner, and the firm of Winter and Pond opened for business at 222 Front Street on July 29, 1893. It operated under their ownership, in various locations, until Pond's death fifty years later. The company enjoyed its heyday before the 1920s.

At the time of Winter and Pond's arrival, Juneau had existed for only twelve years and supported not more than fifteen hundred people.[5] Mining and prospecting were the town's reasons for being; nearly every resident Caucasian owned all or part of a land claim. Many Indians moved to Juneau from their traditional villages to trade or work in mines, settling in a section of town apart from the Caucasians.

Juneau could boast of one hospital, two churches, and three segregated schools: Indian, Catholic, and public. Miners seeking entertainment could choose from perhaps thirty saloons and a number of dance halls and less reputable establishments. The federal government had built a courthouse, but very few public officials were on hand; there was no municipal government and no authority by which one could be organized. Juneau was a community in relative isolation—particularly in winter months when mail and visitors arrived infrequently. Against this backdrop, Lloyd Winter and Percy Pond pursued their fledgling venture. The partners witnessed—and recorded—great changes as Juneau evolved from a mining boomtown into the political capital of a United States territory.

Winter and Pond provided a range of photographic services soon after they opened their business. An advertisement in the May 16, 1894, issue of the *Alaska News* announced, "WINTER & POND . . . The place for the Finest Portraits in Every Style. Old pictures of any kind copied or enlarged and satisfaction guaranteed. Alaska Views."

The following March, an advertisement in the *Alaska Searchlight* read, "Alaska Views. Choicest and largest collection of Views of Alaska Scenery, comprising illustrations of Indian Life, Totems, Glaciers, Seal Islands, Mines, Yukon, Sitka, Juneau, Wrangel and other Points of Interest in Alaska." An advertisement in 1901 emphasized their "Studies of Indian Characters" and "Curios, Totems, Baskets, Silver, Souvenirs, Carvings, Special Indian Calendars and Post Cards." Along with their photographs, the partners sold Native art and for a short time also operated a florist shop in an adjacent building. In April 1916, they offered the "most elaborate assortment" of Easter flowers "ever received in Alaska."[6]

1. Pond was the name of Percy's stepfather. Percy's name at birth was Jaszynsky. His father, originally from Poland, died while Percy was young.
   Information for this biographical sketch, and additional material, can be found in Robert N. De Armond, "Winter and Pond, Photographers, 1893–1956," *Alaska Journal*, Winter 1982, pp. 10–20; and Wendy Calmensen, "Winter and Pond: Pioneer Photographers in Alaska, 1893–1943" (Master's thesis, San Francisco State University, 1979). See also the *Daily Alaska Empire* (Juneau), vol. 66, no. 10 (19 Nov. 1945), pp. 1, 2.

2. Landerking has been variously referred to as Landerkin, Landerkim, Landrigan, and Landiken. I am grateful to Robert N. De Armond (pers. comm., 23 May 1988) for Landerking's naval rank.

3. Among the early photographers in southeast Alaska who took some images before Winter and Pond were C. E. Davison, Edward de Groff, Reuben Albertstone, Brown and Winter (no relation), Frank La Roche, and the Partridges.

4. *Daily Alaska Empire* (Juneau), vol. 60, no. 9289 (12 March 1943), p. 6. Two years later, however, the same newspaper reported that it was Pond who had bought Landerking's share (vol. 66, no. 10 [19 Nov. 1945]), pp. 1, 2.

5. The following description of Juneau in 1893 is based on De Armond, "Winter and Pond," pp. 10–20.

6. *Alaska Record Miner*, 21 June 1901, and *Alaska Daily Empire* (Juneau), 21 April 1916, as cited in Calmensen, "Winter and Pond: Pioneer Photographers in Alaska."

The partners were active in community affairs. At various times, Winter was a member of the Juneau Fire Department, The Arctic Brotherhood, Pioneers of Alaska, Elks, Blue Lodge of Mason, Scottish Rite, Shriners, Order of Eastern Star. He reportedly also served a brief stint in 1901 as Deputy Collector of Customs, stationed in Wrangell.[7] He remained a bachelor his entire life.

Pond, too, joined the fire department, which sponsored sports events, social functions, and holiday celebrations, in addition to fighting blazes. He also served on the Executive Committee of the Juneau Commercial Club, a group of local businessmen, and was a member of the National Woodmen of the World.[8] In 1898 in San Francisco he married Harriet Hall, with whom he had two children. E. P., Jr., and Marian Belle.

By the third decade of the twentieth century, the Winter and Pond studio had passed its prime. The partners continued to do excellent work, but commercial photography had become less profitable. More competition had developed following the Klondike gold rush of 1898, which brought many photographers to Alaska. Technological advances had made photography more accessible to a wider range of people. Tourist travel, which had declined somewhat during the First World War, suffered again during the Depression, and many tourists who did come carried their own cameras.

Despite the quality of its images—and the help of outside backers through incorporation in 1909—the Winter and Pond studio was not a long-term financial success. The partners tried to develop schemes such as tourist excursions to boost their cash flow, but results were not dramatic. Most of the photographs under discussion in this volume were taken during the first fifteen years of the firm's operation.

Percy Pond died June 1, 1943, at the age of 71. In January 1945, Winter turned the business over to an assistant, Francis J. Harrison. Winter died at seventy-nine on November 18, 1945.[9] Harrison continued to run the studio until December 1956. Its closing made front-page news in the *Juneau Independent*, which called it "the oldest business in Alaska."[10]

When Harrison shut down the studio, many of the original negatives were abandoned. The late George Jorgenson, a Juneau resident who had been a friend of Winter and Pond, recovered about 4,700 of the glass plate and nitrate film negatives. In 1981, his son, William Jorgenson, donated this valuable collection to the Alaska State Library. Through his generosity—and a grant from the Alaska State Legislature to print the images—they are now available to researchers and the general public.

The collection embraces a broad spectrum of subjects. When Winter and Pond opened their studio, photography still required bulky equipment and technical knowledge, and only professionals and devoted amateurs owned their own cameras. Most people relied on commercial photographers for photographs. Residents of Juneau, both Caucasian and Indian, came to the partners' studio to sit for their portraits. Settlers long separated from family wanted pictures to send home. Commercial mining companies commissioned photographs of operations and equip-

ment. Local newspapers used images to illustrate stories. Some images, such as those of new buildings, Fourth of July celebrations, and early shipments of automobiles, were primarily of interest to local residents.

In 1899, Winter went to New York to arrange with the national agency of Underwood and Underwood to market Winter and Pond pictures in books, magazines, and other publications. The previous year Winter had served that agency, and the popular publication *Leslie's Weekly*, as a photographer during the Klondike gold rush. Winter and Pond were official Alaska photographers for the Alaska-Yukon-Pacific Exposition in Seattle in 1909. Pond, in charge of collecting photographic views and soliciting contributions of various sorts for exhibitions, reportedly went to the Chilkat country and into the interior, and to Skagway, Berner's Bay, Juneau, Wrangell, and Ketchikan.[11] Since the partners owned their own boat, the *Photo Friday*, they had opportunities to travel to areas off the normal route of the steamships that plied the coast.

Tourists who traveled to Alaska on steamships in the late nineteenth and early twentieth centuries were interested in photographs of their travels. Glaciers, spectacular scenery, and shipwrecks appealed to tourists, and particularly popular were images of the Tlingit and Haida Indians.

Around the turn of the century, photographs of Native Americans generated interest nationwide, and Winter and Pond found themselves in proximity to the rich cultures of the Tlingit and Haida Indians. It was not just the prospect of commercial gain that led them to photograph Indians. They shared a strong interest in the indigenous culture and art. Winter studied the Tlingit language. He and Pond became friends with many Indians, and reportedly were adopted into a Chilkat Tlingit family and received Indian names. They traveled to the upper Lynn Canal area to attend and photograph potlatch celebrations, and apparently were

7. *Daily Alaska Empire,* vol. 66, no. 10,121 (19 Nov. 1945), pp. 1, 2 (formerly the *Alaska Daily Empire*).

8. De Armond, "Winter and Pond," p. 12; *Daily Alaska Dispatch* (Juneau), vol. 48 (9 June 1909), p. 4; *Alaska Daily Empire,* vol. 3, no. 336 (17 Dec. 1913), p. 1; *Daily Alaska Empire,* vol. 61, no. 9359 (2 June 1943), p. 6.

9. *Daily Alaska Empire,* vol. 61, no. 9359 (2 June 1943), p. 6, and vol. 66, no. 10,121 (19 Nov. 1945), pp. 1, 2.

10. *Juneau Independent,* vol. 5, no. 15 (23 Dec. 1956). In making this claim, the newspaper inexplicably dated the founding of the business as 1886, some seven years before Winter and Pond actually arrived on the scene.

11. *Daily Alaska Dispatch,* no. 147 (22 Sept. 1908).

*Percy Pond relaxes in his apartment in a building Winter and Pond erected on South Franklin Street.*

welcome there. Winter's friendships with people from the Chilkat region lasted a lifetime. At his funeral, six Indians served as honorary pallbearers.[12]

Although Winter and Pond did publish some short pamphlets for tourists about Indians and totem poles, they apparently did not intend to produce an organized or comprehensive body of work on Alaskan Indians. Of the approximately 4,700 glass plate and nitrate negatives that were recovered from their studio, only about 400 relate to Indians, their villages and art. Almost all of these date from 1910 or earlier, when the photographers were very active; many such images were still being sold years after they were taken.

While the images of Indians comprise only a small percentage of Winter and Pond's opus, they represent a large and extremely important collection of photographs of Native Alaskans. Although most of Winter and Pond's images of Native peoples were of Tlingit and Haida Indians, the partners did obtain some views of Athabascan Indians and Eskimos.[13] Sometimes photographers who did not concentrate solely on Indians provided the most objective views, since they were less likely to follow a rigid agenda.

Winter and Pond took most of their images of Indians using dry glass plate negatives, a technique that had been introduced in the 1870s. Dry plate negatives were a major improvement over the earlier collodion or wet plate process which dates from 1851. With wet plate negatives, photographers had to carry equipment and chemicals to the field to develop the photographs immediately after they were taken. Dry plate negatives eliminated this problem, and also required somewhat shorter exposures. Subjects still had to stay motionless, but not for as long. Winter and Pond also occasionally used nitrate film negatives.[14]

Even with the glass plate negatives, photography remained cumbersome. Cameras and tripods, although designed to pack neatly into boxes, were heavy to transport, and the negatives were bulky and fragile. Photographers who traveled far afield were burdened by this equipment. The inconvenience helped commercial photographers

12. These men were the Reverend Walter Soboleff, Jack Gamble, Jimmy Fox, Henry Anderson, Jimmy Hanson, and Jake Cropley. *Daily Alaska Empire*, vol. 66, no. 10,124 (23 Nov. 1945), p. 5.

13. These latter groups lie outside the scope of this discussion, which pertains to southeast Alaska.

14. Paula Fleming and Judith Luskey, *The North American Indians in Early Photographs* (New York: Harper and Row, 1986), pp. 14–15. Also see William Crawford, *The Keepers of Light: A History and Working Guide to Early Photographic Processes* (Dobbs Ferry, N.Y.: Morgan and Morgan, 1979), pp. 42–45; and Robert Taft, *Photography and the American Scene: A Social History, 1839–1889* (New York: Dover Publications, 1964), pp. 209, 367–75, 382–83. Film negatives on a nitrocellulose base were introduced to the photography market in the United States around 1890. See Taft, *Photography and the American Scene*, pp. 391–402.

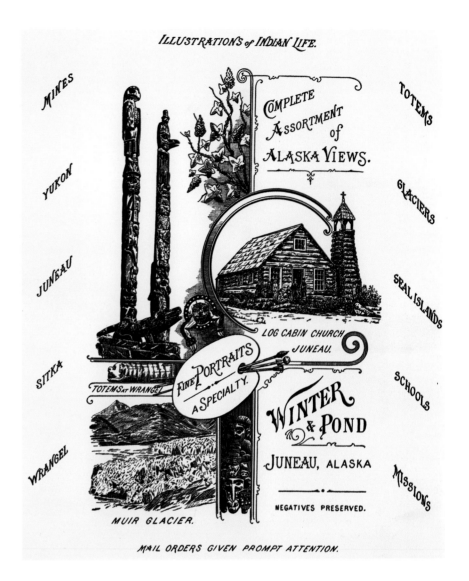

*Like other photographers, Winter and Pond placed advertisements on the back of their cardboard photograph mounts. This one advertises the range of their services, displaying sketches based on their photographs.*

*First built as a residence, this log cabin was used as Juneau's first public school and as a church before becoming a brewery. Here, the church's cross still stands atop the steeple.*

support their industry; as tourists were unable to carry personal cameras easily, they eagerly bought professional images of the places they toured.

Out of their studios, photographers generally relied on natural lighting. When neither natural light nor common forms of artificial lighting were sufficient, magnesium-based flash powder or flash bombs could be ignited to cause a small bright explosion.[15] This technique had drawbacks. Flammable powder had to be carried along with the other equipment. Regulating the intensity, direction, and duration of the flash was difficult. Using too much powder could prove dangerous.

Lighting requirements restricted the images photographers could obtain, since it was difficult to take views such as the dark interiors of Indian longhouses and community houses where dances often were held. Most of Winter and Pond's Indian photographs that were taken beyond the studio depict outdoor scenes. Photographers had to wait for suitable weather, and in southeast Alaska, rain is more the norm than the exception. The glass plate negatives were printed using natural light. The negatives were clamped into a wood frame next to the printing paper, and light passing through the negative burned the image onto the paper.

Winter and Pond sold their commercial views of Indians in regular prints and in postcards. Some of their postcards were hand tinted with pastel colors, in accordance with the common practice of the day. The partners also compiled small albums of photographs for sale. In 1905, their pamphlet *Types of Alaska Natives* appeared. The same year, they copyrighted a brief text about the Indians of southeast Alaska to accompany photographs that were pasted on the pages.[16]

Many of the Winter and Pond images were copyrighted. In some cases, the date of the copyright is written on the glass plate negative. It is not clear whether Winter and Pond regularly filed for a certificate of registration for their prints after they marked the notice of copyright on the negative or print. While in some cases they may have indicated the copyright on the negative some time after the image was created, most dates probably accurately reflect the year the image was taken.[17] Since some of the images were sold over a period of years, negatives occasionally accumulated captions. The captions are helpful, often mentioning the place the photograph was taken or the tribal affiliation of the subject, but they are not invariably reliable. In a few instances, the location cited may be incorrect, or a single image is ascribed at different times to two different locations (see, for example, nos. 20, 35).

Like other commercial photographers of Indians at this time, Winter and Pond rarely mentioned the name of their subject in the caption. Since they had friendships with the Indians and undoubtedly knew names, they must have assumed that this information would not interest white customers. They did not put captions on all their commercial pictures, but they never put captions on private portraits.

Little written documentation exists for the Winter and Pond photographs. Other than the captions and the scanty text in the pamphlets, Winter and Pond did not leave specific information about their images. Since most of the Indian pictures under discussion here were taken almost a century ago, it is difficult to identify the individuals. Oral consultants, Indian and white, were generous with their knowledge and insights. They helped greatly in supplying information about villages, clothing, art pieces, and practices depicted in the photographs. Local newspapers noted Winter and Pond's activities and displayed their advertisements.

Inspection of negatives sometimes uncovers features that do not show in prints. Winter and Pond occasionally used props to convey the impression that an image taken in the studio was actually an outdoors scene. Since some negatives show more of the image than was finally printed, props used for such ruses may be identified and recognized when they appear in other images.

Shading in historical photographs can also be misleading. Black and white glass plate and nitrate negatives used by early photographers were not consistent in the way they recorded colors. Light colors may appear as dark shades of grey, and vice versa; and the same color may appear as different shades of grey in different images. Thus, ethnohistorical photographs are not accurate indicators of the color of clothing and art objects.[18]

The following text, with photographs, is a discussion of how Winter and Pond's images reflect changes in the lives of Tlingit and Haida Indians in southeast Alaska. Additional information about the research and methodology used in interpreting these Winter and Pond photographs can be found in Appendix A. The photographs address values and attitudes in times of transition, often posing more questions than they answer. As they prompt viewers to think about real people and their experiences, the Winter and Pond images assume great value.

15. Taft, *Photography and the American Scene*, p. 201.

16. Lloyd Winter and Percy Pond, *The Totems of Alaska*, unpaginated (New York: The Albertype Company, 1905).

17. Robert N. De Armond, pers. comm., 23 May 1988.

18. See Bill Holm, "Old Photos Might Not Lie, But They Fib a Lot about Color!" *American Indian Art Magazine*, vol. 10, no. 4 (Autumn 1985), pp. 44–49.

Greetings
and
Good Wishes
For a Merry Christmas
and a
Happy New Year.
to


from
An Old Sourdough.

*Lloyd V. Winter.*

*Lloyd Winter prepared a Christmas card with his photograph, proud of his designation as an Alaskan pioneer.*

Canoes on the Chilkat River (enlargement of fig. 64).

RIVER

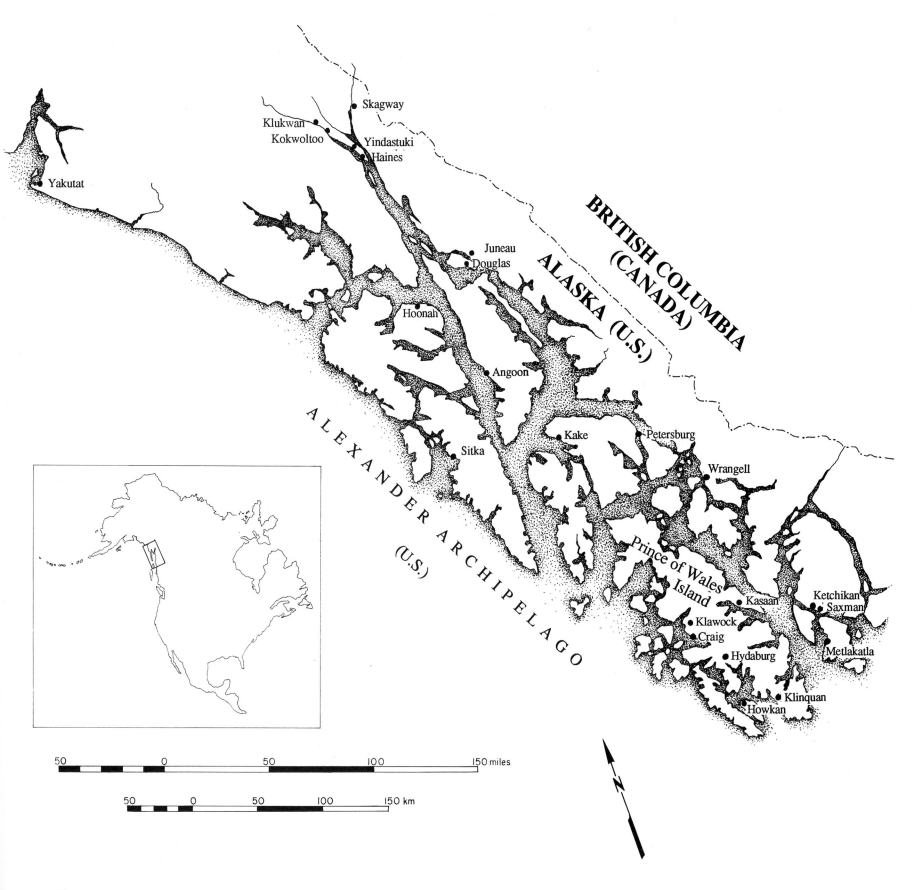

Skagway

Klukwan
Kokwoltoo
Yindastuki
Haines

Yakutat

BRITISH COLUMBIA
(CANADA)

Juneau
Douglas

ALASKA (U.S.)

Hoonah

Angoon

Kake

Petersburg

Sitka

Wrangell

A L E X A N D E R   A R C H I P E L A G O

(U.S.)

Prince of Wales
Island

Kasaan

Ketchikan
Saxman

Klawock

Craig

Hydaburg

Metlakatla

Klinquan

Howkan

| 50 | 0 | 50 | 100 | 150 miles |

| 50 | 0 | 50 | 100 | 150 km |

N

# Images from the Inside Passage

IN THE LATE NINETEENTH AND EARLY TWENTIETH CENTURIES, Tlingit and Haida Indians in southeast Alaska faced extensive changes introduced by foreign settlement. Caucasian settlers brought, among other things, new industries, a new religion, and a new economic system. In the late 1870s, mines and canneries began to open in southeast Alaska. Concomitantly, American missionaries began to arrive. These developments confronted Native people with changes that touched every realm of their lives.

Since few Alaskan Indians left written records at the time, too often their experiences went undocumented. Historical photographs help fill in these gaps. They provide vivid information about the European clothes, architectural innovations, and social activities that Indians incorporated into their lives. Photographs convey a sense of the physical conditions in which many Indians lived, in white towns and in Native villages. Perhaps most important, they make suggestions about Indians' attitudes toward their traditional art and culture during a time of rapid and often painful transition.

Many photographers of American Indians in the late nineteenth century, notably Edward S. Curtis, were most interested in recording Indians as they supposedly looked and lived prior to contact with whites. Anthropologists as well wanted to photograph cultures they believed were disappearing, so that future researchers would have a record of how those people appeared before they were changed forever by contact with white settlers. Commercial photographers were less interested in systematic documentation, but they did seek images their white audiences would find exotic, primitive, even frightening.

Winter and Pond were commercial photographers, and they needed to take pictures that would sell. By the turn of the century in Alaska, Euro-American influences were so widespread that it would have taken fairly extensive staging of photographs to avoid capturing their impact. Many Winter and Pond images of Indians do emphasize traditional art and culture, but almost all show evidence of change due to foreign settlement.

In fact, this may well have been what many of the partners' clients wanted. Tourist traffic to Alaska began in earnest in 1887, when the Pacific Coast Steamship Company initiated summer excursions through the Inside Passage; it continued actively until World War I.[1] The tourists bought images that depicted what they saw—images similar to what they would have taken if they had carried their own cameras.[2] Their expectations were more realistic than those of people who had not traveled in the West. Some photographers who marketed views to easterners sought a romanticized portrayal of Indians; Winter and Pond, who usually sold to a more knowledgeable audience, rarely tried to appeal to nostalgia or tastes for the exotic.

Winter and Pond certainly did consciously orchestrate the content of their pictures. Given their early technology, there was no such thing as a candid photograph. They needed carefully controlled lighting conditions and long exposure times during which subjects had to remain almost motionless. The photographers put much thought into each picture. Whether they were photographing Indians or Caucasians, they arranged their pictures to create certain impressions of their subjects. In some images of Indians, for example, they sought to capture the beauty and drama of a dance, or to recreate a street scene familiar to tourists.

They did not, however, restrict themselves to a single stereotypical image of the Indian. One of the most striking aspects of their collection is that photographs taken in the same time period present so many different images of the local people's conditions. Some show Indians in ragged clothing, sitting on the floor or on the ground (for instance, nos. 11, 32). In vivid contrast, other views show Indians dressed in fashionable and expensive European styles (nos. 13, 14), a far cry from the stereotype most white audiences probably held about Alaskan Indians. Still others present Indians in villages or in the studio dressed in dance outfits or wearing other ceremonial art (nos. 10, 34). Winter and Pond's collection of photographs serves as a rich resource in part because it does present their subjects in so many different lights. They were photographing the conditions of the Indians around them. If almost all of their images of people are staged, only a few are blatantly anachronistic.

1. Robert N. De Armond, "The History of the Sheldon Jackson Museum," in Peter L. Corey, ed., *Faces, Voices and Dreams: A Celebration of the Centennial of the Sheldon Jackson Museum* (Sitka: Alaska State Dept. of Education, and Friends of the Sheldon Jackson Museum, 1987), pp. 3–19.

2. Kodak box cameras and flexible film became available in the late 1880s, but were by no means carried by all tourists in the late nineteenth century.

Outside of the studio, photographers encountered obstacles that influenced the pictures they took. Nonresidents who traveled to Alaska on steamships in the summer had few opportunities to photograph the many Indians who had left their winter villages to work in fishing, mining, and timber industries. In a study of over two hundred photographs relating to Haida Indians, taken between 1878 and 1908, anthropologist Margaret Blackman found that approximately 90 percent showed buildings in permanent winter villages rather than images of people. Photographers who were interested in recording traditional aspects of Native culture could still find totem poles and longhouses to photograph, even if the Indian people dressed like Euro-Americans. Possibly, too, some photographers may have preferred to photograph village landscapes instead of people to avoid having to obtain the cooperation of Indian subjects.[3]

Winter and Pond, in contrast, made regular opportunities to develop lasting friendships with Indians based on their interest in Native culture. They could take pictures that conveyed such disparate impressions of Indians in part because they lived in Alaska. With a studio in Juneau, they obtained portraits unavailable to traveling photographers. Weather permitting, they could travel in any season. They owned a small boat and could visit sites far from the normal steamship routes. Unlike some other photographers, they frequently took village views that featured the Indians (e.g., nos. 45, 47). Included among photographs in the Winter and Pond Collection at the Alaska State Library that show Indians in village contexts are about thirty images from the northern Tlingit villages of Klukwan, Yindastuki, and Kokwoltoo, and a dozen or so more from the Haida villages of Howkan and Klinquan and the Tlingit villages of Kake and Angoon.[4]

# Portraits

Winter and Pond took portraits of Indians indoors and outdoors, in a variety of clothes and dance costumes. Here I will address the setting and posing of these portraits, the selection of subjects, and the variety and significance of costumes. I also consider the manner in which the portraits help reveal the many effects of Euro-American contact on Native Alaskan dress, customs, and economic conditions.

*Lloyd Winter painted portraits as a young man and his interest in drawing stayed with him. Pictured is one of his etchings, based on the accompanying Winter and Pond photograph of an elderly Tlingit woman (facing page).*

3. Margaret B. Blackman, *Window on the Past: The Photographic Ethnohistory of the Northern and Kaigani Haida,* Canadian Ethnology Service Paper No. 74 (Ottawa: National Museums of Canada, 1981), pp. 64, 73.

4. Writers have used several variations of spelling for many Indian villages in southeast Alaska, as well as for other Indian words. Yindaystuckeyah and Yindastuki, for example, are just two of a number of spellings for that village.

The partners took many of their portraits of Indians in their Juneau studio. In the studio setting, they had more control over lighting conditions, and of course did not have to transport their cumbersome photographic equipment. They did have to rely on Indians to come to their studio to be photographed, but many were evidently willing to do so (nos. 4, 9). All the portraits were posed, some stiffly and others more naturally.

Winter and Pond went to considerable trouble to alter their studio in creative ways to provide a variety of environments. They took many of the studio portraits against the painted backdrops common in photographic studios even today—a prop that actually emphasizes the artificial setting (for instance, nos. 3, 12). In other pictures, they created the illusion that the view was taken spontaneously, outside the studio. In these views, they constructed backgrounds of boards, making it appear that their subjects are standing or sitting in front of a building (nos. 17, 18).

Winter and Pond's images reflect standard conventions of portraiture seen in photographs and paintings of the time, a preference reinforced by Winter's experience as a portrait painter. Subjects often rested hands on whatever was available: a friend's shoulder, an artificial fence, even a stump brought in for the purpose. The pictures also suggest that the photographers valued symmetry. They arranged groups of people in pyramid fashion, put similar dance tunics on opposite ends of a photograph, and positioned their subjects so they would harmonize with background features (nos. 12, 21, 67).[5]

Since they were so involved in staging the portraits, it would not have been surprising had Winter and Pond provided dance costumes and art objects with which to pose their subjects—a common enough practice among photographers of American Indians. Sometimes photographers owned ceremonial regalia that they used as props, so the same items appear repeatedly in their photographs. Edward Curtis, the most famous of such photographers, has been criticized for dressing Indian subjects in articles of clothing that actually came from other tribal groups.[6] It is risky to assume that costumes and ceremonial items in historical photographs actually belonged to the person who posed with them.

5. Winter and Pond also photographed whites in the same studio settings, using the same conventions of composition.

6. See, for example, Christopher M. Lyman, *The Vanishing Race and Other Illusions: Photographs of Indians by Edward S. Curtis* (Washington, D.C.: Smithsonian Institution, 1982). For a discussion that forcefully counters many of Lyman's criticisms of Curtis, see Bill Holm's review, "The Vanishing Race and Other Illusions," in *American Indian Art Magazine*, vol. 8, no. 3 (1983), pp. 68–73.

This image shows the variety of arts and crafts that Winter and Pond offered for sale in the "curio shop" they operated in conjunction with their photographic studio. Some of the art objects here, such as the clan hat and the painted bentwood box on which it sits, were made for Native use. Others, such as the model totem poles, were made for tourists. Items for sale include spruce root baskets of many designs, bottles covered with basketry, miniature snowshoes, model canoes, masks, beads, horn spoons, wooden bowls, and carved wood figures. The human figure in the center wears a painted leather dance apron.

With the curio store attached to their photographic studio, Winter and Pond easily could have provided props for their studio portraits. Despite this temptation, they do not seem to have done so very often. Fur capes appear in several of their pictures (nos. 5, 6, 20), and may have been supplied by the photographers, but the same dance costumes do not appear again and again on different individuals. Some of the ceremonial art pieces in the photographs are in museum collections today, and it is known that they belonged to Native caretakers, not to Winter and Pond. Perhaps most telling, few ceremonial art items appear in the studio photographs. To photograph masks, frontlets, helmets, ceremonial rattles, and the other spectacular Tlingit and Haida dance regalia, Winter and Pond usually went to the Indian villages. Indians may have brought ceremonial dancing blankets and tunics to the Juneau studio, but they did not often travel there with their other ceremonial items.

By Winter and Pond's time, Indians in southeast Alaska had long been wearing European clothing. Wool cloth and ready-made clothing were introduced to these Indians by maritime fur traders in the late eighteenth and early nineteenth centuries. As early as 1869, Frederick W. Seward, the son of Secretary of State William Seward, visited the relatively remote Chilkat region and reported that the Indians there had discarded "savage dress." Aurel Krause, who was there in 1881, noted that "the aboriginal costume can no longer be found anywhere among the Tlingit."[7] Winter and Pond did not try to hide the fact that Indians wore white-style clothing. Only the posed scenes of the doctor Skundoo (one shown here, no. 26) show no evidence of commercial clothes. Skundoo appears in another image in coat and trousers (no. 25).

Even in their studio portraits, Winter and Pond show Indians in a variety of circumstances. Some subjects dress entirely in dance regalia or cover street clothes with dance tunics or ceremonial button blankets. Others wear dressy clothing, with no trace of dance regalia that emphasizes their ethnic heritage. Still others wear very worn clothes, draped with wool blankets. The women often wear head kerchiefs. These striking contrasts reflect the fact that there was no "typical" Indian in southeast Alaska. While most did struggle with the limited economic opportunities available to Indians, some were able to afford expensive clothes pictured in a few of the photographs.

Some of the Winter and Pond studio views respond to tourist attitudes toward Indians, or otherwise give insights into Indian-white relations at the time. In a few images, the photographers recreated scenes that tourists were likely to encounter on the streets (nos. 17, 21, 22). They posed women to appear to be waiting to sell curios to tourists. Women selling baskets, small wood carvings, and other "curios" were a common scene in the summer in towns up and down the coast of southeast Alaska. Indian women lined the docks to meet passengers who disembarked from the steamships that plied an active tourist trade.

In 1908, one traveler on the steamships wrote, "There is no night so wild and tempestuous, and no hour of any night so late, or of any morning so early, that the passenger hastening ashore is not greeted by this long line of dark-faced women. They sit like so many patient, noiseless statues, with their tempting wares clustered around the flat, 'toed-in' feet of each." The same writer added that the women had a droll sense of humor, "and one is sure to have considerable fun poked at one, going down the line." Income from the sale of baskets and other curios was especially important to Indian women, who did not have as much opportunity as men to earn money in the industries introduced by American entrepreneurs.[8]

Pictures of women selling curios to tourists are fairly common, probably because these views were easily accessible to photographers who traveled on the steamships themselves. Winter and Pond preferred to recreate these scenes in their controlled studio setting. Sometimes they clearly posed these images (for example, no. 21), but at other times they introduced a false wall to simulate the outdoors (no. 20).

The captions Winter and Pond chose also shed light on white attitudes toward Indians. Identifying the subject as "Doctor" or "Medicine Man"— what Tlingits called an *ixt*—sparked commercial interest.[9] Among their own people, these ixts, usually male, traditionally were believed to have extraordinary communication with certain spirits, giving them the power to cure illness or to detect witches. (In the early 1880s, ixts in the Chilkat region charged ten blankets to cure sick people.[10])

7. Frederick W. Seward, "Eclipse at Chilkat," *Alaska Journal*, vol. 2, no. 1 (1973), pp. 18–20; Aurel Krause, *The Tlingit Indians: Results of a Trip to the Northwest Coast of America and the Bering Straits*, translated by Erna Gunther (Seattle: University of Washington Press, 1956), p. 101.

8. Ella Higginson, *Alaska: The Great Country* (New York: Macmillan Company, 1908), pp. 190–91. For more discussion of Native responses to Caucasian industries, see Victoria Wyatt, "Alaskan Indian Wage Earners in the 19th Century: Economic Choices and Ethnic Identity on Southeast Alaska's Frontier," *Pacific Northwest Quarterly*, vol. 78, nos. 1–2 (1987), pp. 43–49. Wyatt discusses the impact of the tourist markets on Northwest Coast Indian arts in her *Shapes of Their Thoughts: Reflections of Culture Contact in Northwest Coast Indian Art* (New Haven: Yale Peabody Museum of Natural History and University of Oklahoma Press, 1984).

9. Frederica de Laguna includes an extensive discussion of Tlingit shamanism in *Under Mount Saint Elias: The History and Culture of the Yakutat Tlingit*, Smithsonian Contributions to Anthropology, vol. 7, pp. 670–725.

10. Caroline Willard, 13 Dec. 1881, to "My Dear Friends,"in Eva McClintock, ed., *Life in Alaska: Letters of Mrs. Eugene S. Willard* (Philadelphia: Presbyterian Board of Education, 1884), p. 131.

Missionaries were adamantly opposed to ixts, whom they felt represented a competing belief system. Since ixts and their clients believed that an ixt's power disappeared if his hair was cut, missionaries could stop individual ixts from practicing even if they could not prevent clients from believing in the concept. In the late nineteenth century, when one ixt from Hoonah refused to stop practicing, Presbyterian missionary S. Hall Young forcibly cut his hair. Young explained: "He threatened to kill himself in order that his family might collect damages, but when, instead of imploring him to remain alive, I encouraged him in his suicidal intention, saying that the country would be better without him, he concluded to spite me by continuing to exist." Ixts were correct to feel seriously threatened by missionaries, and many opposed the foreigners strongly. As late as 1909, a missionary in Hoonah complained that ixts still practiced there.[11]

Ixts were popular subjects for commercial photographers, who rightly guessed that white audiences would be intrigued by the images. Winter and Pond took several pictures of people they identified as "Doctor" or "Medicine Man" (see nos. 23, 26, 27), not all of whom necessarily were.

If chiefs and ixts were popular images to sell to tourists, so were Indian children. Winter and Pond knew well that babies and young children have universal appeal, and they took several views of children posed together (nos. 12, 17, 18). They made an image of a sleeping baby into a Christmas card (no. 28).

The changes in Indians' economic activities as a result of contact were rarely recorded on film. Contemporary anthropologists appear to have been more interested in documenting aspects of traditional culture than in studying Indians who worked in white industries, and commercial photographers, in addition to their difficulty in getting proper lighting for images taken indoors, probably considered other views more marketable. Winter and Pond were able to visit summer fishing camps and canneries that were off the normal route of photographers who traveled on summer steamships. Their views of an Indian fishing camp (for example, nos. 37, 38), taken in the summer of 1894, are particularly unusual. These views provide valuable evidence of the mix of utensils used at the camp—some of which were of Native design and some of which were bought in stores—and give a vivid impression of what life on the beach was like.

Another unusual photograph, entitled "The Labeler" (no. 36), shows an Indian woman working indoors at a cannery near Sitka, putting labels on salmon cans. Winter and Pond's image is one of the few that exist as visual records of work inside a cannery. The first salmon canneries in southeast Alaska opened in the late 1870s. Many Alaskan Indians were eager to earn wages in these industries, and traveled to cannery sites in the summer to work. Especially in the early years of their enterprises here, American industrialists depended to some extent on Native-American labor for a work force. This economic reality distinguished

Alaska from the other regions of the American West where whites had moved into Indian lands, for in Alaska, although they appropriated important salmon streams, the settlers did not force Indians away from the regions they settled.

Working for the canneries, Indian men often fished; women generally had the indoor jobs: washing the fish, preparing them for canning, and putting labels on the cans. In 1890 at one cannery in southeast Alaska, men earned one dollar and fifty cents per day for washing and preparing the salmon, while women earned one dollar a day for the same task.[12]

Whether indoors or outdoors, the photographers put considerable care into the composition of their images. Winter and Pond needed the cooperation and patience of their subjects in order to pose the photograph. Long exposure times made spontaneous shots impossible. Most portraits taken outdoors were no more candid than those taken in the studio.

# Villages, Totem Poles, and Architecture

Like other photographers in turn-of-the-century Alaska, Winter and Pond were interested in photographing Indian villages with their distinctive communal longhouses and dramatic art. Since they revisited some villages, their views show changes over time. The villages they photographed included the Tlingit settlements in Klukwan, Yindastuki, Kokwoltoo, Juneau (Auk), Sitka, Wrangell, and Kake, and the Haida villages of Howkan and Klinquan.

Before the arrival of Europeans, Indians in southeast Alaska lived in villages scattered in well over a dozen remote locations throughout an archipelago five hundred miles long. Each village was politically autonomous, and people from different villages traded with each other, intermarried, and also raided and battled each other. Having developed the technology to store salmon caught in summer at temporary fish camps, the Indians did not constantly need to travel after food in winter. They could establish permanent villages, with huge houses and monumental structures.

11. S. Hall Young, *Hall Young of Alaska, "The Mushing Parson": The Autobiography of S. Hall Young* (New York and Chicago: Fleming H. Revell Co., 1927), p. 155; Rev. A. J. Whipkey, "Last Winter at Hoonah," *Assembly Herald*, vol. 15, no. 6 (1909), pp. 269–70.

12. Patricia Roppel, "Loring," *Alaska Journal*, vol. 5, no. 3 (Summer 1975), pp. 169–78.

Showing the humorous side of Winter and Pond, this photograph records a surveying scene in which a beer bottle tops the surveying equipment. Less humorous is the restaurant's sign, which reflects the prejudice Indians and other ethnic groups faced during Juneau's frontier days.

Villages had a long string of communal houses along a shoreline, facing the water. Some of the structures, known today as longhouses or bighouses, housed related families; others were reserved for ceremonial activities. The rectangular interior was one large room, sometimes enclosing as much as 2,500 square feet, with a central fire pit and a smoke hole in the roof. Traditionally there were no windows or hinged doors, although loosely fitting timbers in the walls and ceiling allowed for some light and ventilation. Interior house posts held up the heavy roof beams, and totem poles often stood in front of the houses, carved with figures that designated the lineage of the owners of the house. While changes had come by the 1890s when Winter and Pond were active, the photographers knew the dramatic totem poles and longhouses would still appeal to tourists. They took some spectacular pictures. (Numbers 71 and 76 are good examples).

When Wrangell, Juneau, and other towns became business centers, Indians from many villages moved there to trade and work in new industries such as mines and canneries. Indians modified their architecture. Winter and Pond were not seeking to record these changes, but they could not help recording them when they made images of villages.

I n the last quarter of the nineteenth century, Alaskan Indians began incorporating some aspects of Euro-American architecture into their buildings. Initially these innovations were restricted to cosmetic changes to the front of the house. They sometimes painted the front a solid color, added trim to the cornice, or even created a new house front from milled lumber.[13] The interior of the houses remained essentially unchanged.

The most prevalent modification of longhouse fronts was the addition of paned glass windows and hinged doors with frames. Indians brought their windows and doors from general merchants who operated stores for whites and Indians. In 1880 and 1881, John Green Brady, who operated a mercantile store in Sitka, sold "many windows" to Indians. He reported that they also purchased carpentry tools, and were interested in lumber.[14] Only Indians who could afford to buy these items could add windows and doors to their houses. Their desire to do so was one reason many were interested in earning wages in the new industries.

The Winter and Pond photographs show the kinds of windows available at the time. Particularly favored were tall windows, sometimes almost three-quarters of the height of the door, which were hung level with the top of the door, or slightly above it. Windows were always placed symmetrically, with either one or two on each side of the door, in accordance with the emphasis on symmetry in Northwest Coast Indian art. Sometimes a window was added directly above the door. This may have served to give the illusion of a second story,[15] but some of these

high windows were accessible from the inside of the house. Windows on the sides of communal longhouses were rare. Margaret Blackman has pointed out that the fronts of longhouses were sometimes traditionally decorated for status purposes, and that the addition of windows to the front may have served a similar function.

These architectural changes came more slowly to outlying villages than they did to villages closer to white settlement. The Sitka *Alaskan* of December 5, 1885, reported that almost all the Indian houses in Sitka, a town with a relatively large white population, were being built "in the white style." However, Winter and Pond's photographs from the relatively remote Chilkat villages of Klukwan, Yindastuki and Kokwoltoo, taken ten years later, show that only some of the houses had had windows or milled lumber added to facades.

Some Indians replaced their communal longhouses with single-family homes. Missionaries, teachers, and government officials encouraged them in this, and also pressured them to stop raising totem poles and carved burial monuments. In June 1881, Navy Commander Henry Glass reported with satisfaction that in the previous four months Indians had built seven new single-family homes.[16] When Presbyterian missionaries Eugene and Caroline Willard arrived in the Chilkat country in the summer of 1881, Chief Don-a-wok, a leading man about sixty years old in the village of Yindastuki, told them that he hoped to build an American house "with an upstairs" if he could obtain the lumber. Six years later, Governor Alfred P. Swineford noted that "as fast as [Indians] can accumulate the means they tear down their old houses and build new ones of more modern style."[17]

13. For discussion of changes in architecture among Haida Indians in British Columbia and Alaska, see Margaret B. Blackman, "Creativity in Acculturation: Art, Architecture and Ceremony from the Northwest Coast," in *Ethnohistory*, vol. 23, no. 4 (Fall 1976), pp. 387–413.

14. John Green Brady to Sheldon Jackson, 29 Jan. 1882, Brady Papers, Beinecke Rare Book and Manuscript Library, Yale University.

15. See Blackman, "Creativity in Acculturation," pp. 402–4.

16. Commander Henry Glass to Secretary of the Navy, 6 June 1881. "Commanders' Letters 1881 Navy Department," National Archives, Code M 147, Roll 116.

17. Caroline Willard to parents, 24 Aug. 1881, in McClintock, ed., *Life in Alaska*, p. 68; Alfred P. Swineford, "Report of the Governor of Alaska to the Secretary of the Interior, 1887" (Washington, D.C.: U.S. Government Printing Office, 1887). Chief Don-a-wok is identified by Aurel Krause in *The Tlingit Indians*, p. 94.

Some of these houses are seen in Winter and Pond's photographs. The one best known was built in 1887 by Kadishan, a leading man in Wrangell (nos. 49, 50). Kadishan had been friendly toward Presbyterian missionaries in Wrangell when the first mission opened in 1877. The Reverend S. Hall Young called him "the shrewdest and most diplomatic of the stikens [sic]." Kadishan accompanied Young and naturalist John Muir on their northern explorations in 1879, and probably helped give speeches about Christianity at Indian villages.[18] The July 23, 1887, issue of the *Alaskan* reported:

An Indian named Kadishan is having built a two-storey residence on the site of his old house, with two sets of bay windows above and below. The building is a frame one covered with rustic with building paper under it. It will be finished inside with lumber and looks as if it will be one of the nicest in the country. Beat that if you can.[19]

In his annual report for 1887, Governor Swineford described the house as "the finest and most pretentious private residence I have seen anywhere in the territory."[20] Kadishan kept his totem poles standing in their traditional location in front of his house. In adopting foreign architecture, he did not reject his Native heritage.

Winter and Pond photographs also show other Native houses that depart from traditional architecture. In a view of the Haida village of Howkan (no. 48), the largest whitewashed house has a totem pole in front of it. This house belonged to Moses Kulthgid, and is said to have been used for community gatherings.[21] The roof line of the smaller house near it shows influence of Euro-American architecture.

Indians used house fronts to display cultural messages. The photographs show that house owners continued to use fronts for this purpose when they added innovations inspired by foreign contact. Occasionally, traditional Haida and Tlingit house fronts were painted with crest designs. In an unwritten language, the painting on the house front declared information about the lineage of some of the people it sheltered. After architectural innovations became popular, some new items began to be displayed on them. One Winter and Pond scene shows a plaque resembling the United States bald eagle symbol hanging above the door of an Indian house (no. 35). Another photograph showing a plaque, in Howkan, is not included here. These plaques were probably manufactured by non-Indians.

Sometimes Indians introduced the use of English language into this longstanding tradition of display. They placed written plaques on their house fronts that served a similar role to that of the crest art: to testify to the lineage of the current owner. Such written plaques also conveyed information about the accomplishments and status of the owner. Often the verses seemed to be oriented toward white audiences, who would not understand messages conveyed by crest design.

Winter and Pond photographed houses in the Tlingit village of Killisnoo (see pp. 32 and 33) belonging to two rival leaders, Kachuckte and Saginaw Jake (Kitchnath). Kachuckte's plaque refers to an event in October of 1882, when Indians in the nearby village of Angoon took custody of some white men because Indians had not received compensation for relatives killed in accidents while working for the Northwest Trading Company. After a series of complex events, Commander E. C. Merriman of the United States Navy warned the Indians to vacate their houses and had the U.S. Revenue Cutter *Corwin* shell the vacant village. Forty canoes and all but four houses were destroyed. Angoon Indians moved to Killisnoo after the event.[22]

Both plaques appear to speak to whites. Kachuckte in particular seemed eager to express his goodwill and lack of hostility toward whites. Actually a leader of the village of Neltushkin, about twelve miles from Killisnoo, he owned a house at Angoon but was not there during the bombing. According to Commander Merriman, Saginaw Jake took 160 blankets from Kachukte's house after the bombing, some of which he presented to Merriman. Despite Kachuckte's words of goodwill, he was feared by whites who lived in Killisnoo.[23]

18. S. Hall Young, *Autobiography*, pp. 184–86.

19. As cited by Edward L. Keithahn in *Monuments in Cedar: The Authentic Story of the Totem Pole* (New York: Bonanza Books, 1963), p. 47.

20. Swineford, "Report . . . to the Secretary of the Interior, 1887."

21. Margaret B. Blackman, pers. comm., 12 Sept. 1987.

22. Frederica de Laguna discusses the bombing of Angoon in *The Story of a Tlingit Community: A Problem in the Relationship Between Archaeological, Ethnological and Historical Methods* (Washington, D.C.: U.S. Government Printing Office, 1960); see also Caroline Willard, letter to parents, 24–30 Oct. 1882, in McClintock, ed., *Life in Alaska*, pp. 236–39; and William T. Lopp, "Report on the Education of the Natives of Alaska and the Reindeer Service," Report of the Commissioner of Education for 1910 (Washington, D.C.: U.S. Government Printing Office), p. xv (also in 61st Cong., 3rd Sess., H.R. Doc. 1006, Ser. 5978). As Ted C. Hinckley notes in "A New Perspective on the Navy's Destruction of the Tlingit Indian Village of Angoon in 1882" (paper delivered at the Eighth Naval History Symposium, U.S. Naval Academy, 25 Sept. 1987), in 1974 the United States paid reparations for the destruction of Angoon. Information in Robert N. De Armond's communication of 23 May 1988 has also contributed to my discussion.

23. Robert N. De Armond, pers. comm., 23 May 1988.

The wording on Saginaw Jake's plaque reads:

By the Gouvernors Commission,
And the Companys Permission,
I am made the grand Tyhee,
Of this entire Illahee.

Prominent in song and story,
I've attained the top of glory.
As Saginaw, I'm known to fame,
Jake is but my common name.

*Winter and Pond posed Saginaw Jake (left) and Kahchucte (facing page) in front of their respective houses, wearing symbols of their prestigious positions on the federal government's Native police force. The photographs record the men's response to the destruction of Angoon, which took place over a decade before, showing how they used their homes to display information.*

Kachuckte's plaque seems to answer Jake's:

Rightfull chief of all "Neltusken,"
"Gungh," "Tah-koogh," and "Koochka-heen."
Known as such, I am, "Kah-chuckte,"
From Yakutat to far Stickeen.

Yes, my name it is "Kah-chuckte."
Manslayer, in the Boston tongue.
Old as yonder granite mountains
Is the lineage whence I sprang.

Stores of furs and blankets pillaged,
By the "Adams" pirate crew.
Though "Kah-chuckte," ever neutral,
Dwelt afar from "Kootznahoo."

Now I ask not for possitions.
Such to Jake I will concede.
While "Kah-chuckte," from your nation,
Will, for justice only, plead.

Totem poles were another means of presenting information about status and lineage. Indians raised them for a variety of reasons, including to mark the genealogy of the owners of a house and to honor someone who recently died. Totem poles were commissioned from master carvers, who were paid for their work. It took years of study and apprenticeship to develop the skill to carve the sculptures.

The carved images on the poles are usually animal figures that represent crest designs. As Winter and Pond themselves emphasized in their pamphlet *The Totems of Alaska*, the crest images were not worshipped as gods. An individual belonged to a clan that displayed a crest design as its symbol, similar to a coat of arms. Families claimed ancestral connections with animal spirits to whom they were related in bygone times—or with whom their ancestors had significant encounters—and the crest designs of these animals linked individuals with their traditional history.[24]

Winter and Pond appreciated Alaskan Indian art and culture, but they shared some of the prejudices of their time. Like most of their white contemporaries, they did not fully recognize the sophistication of the Northwest Coast Indian art styles. In *The Totems of Alaska*, they called the totem poles "rude carvings" and referred to their "uncouth and barbarous appearance."[25] On the other hand, in the same pamphlet they spoke highly of the distinctive two-dimensional art: "Emblazoned on treasure chests, wrought in articles of every day use, painted on the exteriors and interiors of houses, woven into basketry and the famous Chilkat blanket are designs showing a high order of artistic conception and execution."

Winter and Pond photographed some magnificent examples of Tlingit and Haida sculpture and design. Some of the poles may have been forty or fifty years old, and give a clear impression of the appearance of classic carvings erected in the early nineteenth century. The partners also photographed new poles, showing developments in the latter part of the century. Today, researchers are studying carving styles to identify the works of individual artists and to determine how widely they practiced. Historical photographs of poles help greatly in this effort.

Native graveyards were popular subjects for Winter and Pond because these sites displayed grave houses and monumental totem poles and sculptures carved with crest designs honoring the deceased. Some of the grave houses and totem poles actually contained ashes or bones; others served as monuments. Christian missionaries were eager to encourage Indians to abandon their burial practices and adopt Christian burials and gravestones.

By the 1880s, Indians in some villages were incorporating European influences into their burial sites. While cremation was their normal procedure, Tlingit Indians did begin to bury some bodies. They erected white picket fences around some grave sites and decorated mortuary houses with elaborate lathe work. Some of the Winter and Pond images show Indian burial sites in transition, with monumental poles and sculptures next to Christian-style graves (nos. 59, 60, 61).

# Ceremonies and Art

Among the most dramatic forms of Native cultural expression in southeast Alaska were the celebrations known today as potlatches. Potlatches—and the feasts, dancing, and distribution of gifts they included—commemorated important events such as the dedication of a house, the raising of a totem pole, a marriage, a death, or the assumption of a new name or position of leadership. In the absence of a written language, potlatches provided a forum in which people could publicly confirm commitments and rights. By witnessing the distribution of gifts and accepting those gifts, potlatch participants validated the host's claim to privileges. People who received gifts at potlatches maintained their honor by hosting their own potlatches during which they returned the generosity.[26]

Myths, family histories, genealogies, and other cultural information were also passed from generation to generation at potlatches. Songs and dances reenacted ancestral experiences with spirits, and recalled individuals' links with their families. Families owned the right to sing certain songs and perform specific dances—privileges that could be inherited or granted as part of a dowry.

In potlatches, dancers wore spectacular ceremonial costumes. Chilkat dancing blankets and tunics woven in elaborate designs from mountain goat wool and cedar bark, wool blankets emblazoned with crest designs outlined in pearl buttons or dentalia, and cuffs and neck ornaments of intricate beadwork made colorful clothing as dancers swayed. Helmets, masks, frontlets, and clan hats skillfully carved from wood displayed the crests of the wearer. Artists made dramatic use of a variety of materials, adorning the wood with abalone shell, feathers, ermine skins, human hair, paint, and copper highlights. Spruce root hats with painted designs also presented crests. Rattles and drums added sound, and singers provided music for the dancers.

24. For more discussion of totem poles, see Halpin, *Totem Poles: An Illustrated Guide*; and Marius Barbeau, *Totem Poles* (Ottawa: National Museums of Canada, Bulletin 119, 1950), 2 vols.

25. Winter and Pond did mention the "excellence" of the miniature argillite totem poles of the Haida Indians on the Queen Charlotte Islands in British Columbia.

26. For a concise discussion of ceremonies, ancestral connections, and mythology on the Northwest Coast, see Halpin, *Totem Poles: An Illustrated Guide*, pp. 5–15. A comprehensive discussion of types of potlatches, and bibliography on the potlatch, can be found in de Laguna, *Under Mount Saint Elias*, pp. 606–51.

With so much spectacular art, potlatches made particularly dramatic subject matter for photographers. It was not easy for photographers to take photographs of potlatches, however, and relatively few images exist. Up and down the Northwest Coast, white authorities suppressed the potlatch. This suppression caused considerable hardship, since the potlatch was such an important cultural and economic institution.

In British Columbia, the ceremonies were outlawed by the Canadian government in 1884.[27] Subsequently some potlatches were held in secret. In Alaska, there was no legislation proscribing potlatches. They continued in some places beyond the turn of the century despite strong efforts on the part of government officials, missionaries, and schoolteachers to discourage them. These whites felt the potlatch competed with Christianity, and they were also concerned that it left the hosts without money. In January 1902, Governor John Green Brady described his view of a recent potlatch in the Chilkat region:

These are hardworking self supporting people but some of their customs keep them on a low plane. The potlatch is a ceremony which a head man goes through in giving away all his property save his house, canoe and gun. Bales of blankets are torn into strips, bolts of calico and brown sheeting into fathoms and handed out as each name is called, hundreds of cases of pilot bread, barrels of sugar, rice, apples, etc. etc. There were $17,000 spent at one potlatch last year at Chilcat when several head men joined.[28]

Brady noted that the guests were invited "from all the settlements," and were expected to give return potlatches. He felt this practice "dissipated" their savings and prevented them from improving their material standard of living.

In 1904, Governor Brady helped organize a ceremony in Sitka that was meant to be a final potlatch. Leaders there agreed to pay off all debts and eliminate obligations to sponsor any future dances. Potlatches continued in remote villages. As late as 1909, the Reverend A. J. Whipkey, a Presbyterian missionary at the Tlingit village of Hoonah, lamented that potlatch feasts still continued there.[29] In some villages, variations of potlatching survived all the pressure exerted to suppress them. Fortunately, potlatch traditions are being revived today.

Given the pressure against potlatches, they were not widely advertised, and photographers did not always hear of the events. Even when they did, traveling to the sites was not often easy. Potlatches were traditionally held in the winter months, so were missed by commercial photographers who were only present in the summer. By the last decade of the nineteenth century, when Alaskan photography was increasing, potlatch activities were most prevalent in the remote villages where Indians had been less pressured by disapproving Caucasian communities.[30]

Even if photographers could get to the location of the potlatch, they had to obtain the cooperation of the participants. This was much more than a courtesy. Guests at potlatches were expected to have been invited by the host. Most potlatch activities took place indoors and dancers had to be willing to pose outdoors for the photograph, or to submit to flash powder or flash bombs inside the longhouse. In either event, they had to stand still during the exposure. No photographer could take a marketable photograph of a potlatch without the knowledge and cooperation of the participants.

Photographs of potlatches in Alaska were generally taken by resident photographers, such as Winter and Pond or E. W. Merrill, who probably knew some of the potlatch participants. These photographers still could not take cooperation for granted. The April 2, 1897, issue of the *Alaskan* (page 1), noted the following about Sitka photographer Edward de Groff:

Surely the noble red man is making rapid strides toward civilization. Recently an Indian dance was going on in the ranch and our enterprising artist, deGroff, rushed over with his instrument all cocked and primed to take in the situation. On his arrival at the scene of action he was informed by the Alaskan Yankees that he must pay for the privilege of taking their picture for the reason that when they go to his place he charges them for taking their picture, and as he has come to their place he must pay them."

The paper added that "needless to say" de Groff refused to pay, and that the summer tourists would not be able to see pictures of the dance.

Under these circumstances, Winter and Pond may have been lucky to get some of their potlatch photographs. They enjoyed opportunities to photograph potlatches because they lived in Alaska year-round, and because they had a comfortable relationship with many Indians. As very close friends of a Chilkat Tlingit family, they may have gained access to some events in Chilkat villages that were not so easily visited by other photographers. Even if they did not often photograph potlatches, they got dramatic images from those they did record. There is no record as to whether they paid for the opportunity to photograph Indians at potlatches. Some potlatch participants may have welcomed having the

27. For a discussion of the prohibition of the potlatch in British Columbia, see Forrest E. La Violette, *The Struggle for Survival: Indian Cultures and the Protestant Ethic in British Columbia* (Toronto: University of Toronto Press, 1961), pp. 43–97. *Prosecution or Persecution*, by the Kwakiutl author Daisy (My-yah-nelth) Sewid-Smith, relates Native testimony and official correspondence about the law (British Columbia: Nu-Yum-Baleess Society, 1979).

28. Governor Brady to the U.S. Secretary of the Interior, 6 Jan. 1902, in Brady Papers, Beinecke Rare Books and Manuscript Library, Yale University.

29. Ted C. Hinckley describes this "final" potlatch in *Alaskan John G. Brady: Missionary, Businessman, Judge, and Governor, 1878–1918* (N.p.: Miami University by Ohio State University Press, 1982), pp. 249–53; Rev. A. J. Whipkey, "Last Winter at Hoonah," pp. 269–70.

30. For more discussion of why photographs of potlatches are rare, see Blackman, *Window on the Past*, p. 73.

ceremonial occasions recorded on film. At potlatches, certain claims were validated by the presence of witnesses. The photograph preserved the event on paper similar to the way that it was preserved in the memories of the living witnesses.[31]

Particularly striking are Winter and Pond's photographs of Klukwan, probably taken together in the winter of 1894–95. Although the two had been in Alaska for only a year or so, they had lost no time in developing good relations with the Indians and gaining entrée to ceremonial events. Their images include a series of views of the interior of the Whale House at Klukwan (nos. 72, 73), which belonged to the Gaanaxteidi clan under the care of the clan's leader Yeilgooxu, known in English as George Shotridge. The ceremonial house sheltered some of the finest examples of northern Northwest Coast Indian art, including the elaborately carved and painted Rain Screen, several house posts, and a sculpture of a mythical Woodworm. In 1881, missionary Caroline Willard reported that the carvings in some of Shotridge's houses were worth thousands of blankets. Since blankets cost three to four dollars each in the Chilkat country, the carvings represented a very high financial investment for the 1880s.[32]

Winter and Pond took several pictures of people and art arranged inside the Whale House (see no. 73), and more outdoors of posed dancers in ceremonial regalia (no. 66). These photographers were not ethnographers trying to record specific dances, and therefore authenticity was not their objective. In fact, there is some evidence of clowning. In photograph number 65, a boy wears a basketry hat cover as if it were a hat, and in number 72, the man emerging from the hole in the dance screen wears around his neck the leather wings seen in number 65. The images do show art objects being worn as they would have been displayed in animation. The vitality of the occasion comes through clearly in the photograph, and in the days before movie cameras, this imagery was the best way to capture the atmosphere of the dance.

The art pieces in the Klukwan Whale House have at various times been the object of conflict—between collectors who wished to purchase them and clan members who were unwilling to part with them at any price. Louis Situwuka Shotridge, the son of George Shotridge, attempted to purchase the sculptures in the 1920s for The University Museum at the University of Pennsylvania. Since lines of inheritance were matrilineal, he lacked ownership rights, and he could not induce clan members to sell.[33] In recent years, ownership of the spectacular art objects has again been at issue.

Winter and Pond later photographed a procession of dancers in Chilkat blankets and frontlets (no. 77). The photographers marketed one such image under the name "Chilkat Dancers," but it was actually taken in Klinquan, a Haida village on Prince of Wales Island far to the south of the Tlingit Chilkat region. Contemporary residents of Hydaburg have identified the Haida marchers in the picture.[34]

Anthropologist Ronald Weber suggests that the crests on many of the art objects photographed in Klinquan are not appropriate to the lineage of the wearers, and anthropologist Peter Macnair has pointed out that—among other inconsistencies—a rattle was never normally used to beat a drum.[35] Weber concludes that the art is not being displayed in a traditional way, and that the entire procession was staged for the photographers. The images show that those objects were being displayed, whether or not within a traditional cultural context, and that for some reason the subjects were willing to be photographed wearing them.

The Klinquan marchers wear dressy commercial clothes. One man has a vest and watch chain under his Chilkat blanket. The dancers at the Klukwan potlatch also wear European clothes under their regalia. This follows naturally since European dress had long been the normal wear. The potlatch participants felt no compulsion to eliminate practices they had adopted from foreigners before conducting time-honored ceremonies. They were not attempting nostalgically to recreate activities of a bygone time, but were performing ceremonies that had significance in their present lives.

31. In her Foreword to Ulli Steltzer, *A Haida Potlatch* (Seattle: University of Washington Press, 1984), p. x, Marjorie Halpin alludes to the use of the camera in "witnessing."

32. Caroline Willard to Sheldon Jackson, 12 Sept. 1881, and to "My Dear Friends," 13 Dec. 1881, in McClintock, ed., *Life in Alaska*, pp. 78–79, 131. One of the houses to which she was referring was the Whale House (see nos. 71, 72, 73). The Rain Screen—a spectacular carved and painted wooden partition from behind which dancers appeared during ceremonies—is illustrated in these images. For more information on the Whale House, see George T. Emmons, "The Whale House of the Chilkat," *Anthropological Papers of the American Museum of Natural History*, vol. 19, no. 1 (1916), pp. 1–33.

33. For more discussion of Louis Shotridge's attempts to obtain the Whale House art, see Maureen Milburn, "Louis Shotridge and the Objects of Everlasting Esteem," in Susan Kaplan and Kristin Barsness, *Raven's Journey: The World of Alaska's Native People* (Philadelphia: The University Museum, University of Pennsylvania, 1986), pp. 54–77; and Edmund Carpenter's "Introduction," in Bill Holm and Bill Reid, *Indian Art of the Northwest Coast: A Dialogue on Craftsmanship and Aesthetics* (Seattle: University of Washington Press, 1976), pp. 17–24. Douglas Cole discusses Shotridge in *Captured Heritage: The Scramble for Northwest Coast Artifacts* (Seattle: University of Washington Press; Vancouver: Douglas and McIntyre, 1985), pp. 254–67.

34. Identifications, and the current locations of the art pieces in the photographs, are discussed in more detail by Ronald L. Weber in "Photographs as Ethnographic Documents," *Arctic Anthropology*, vol. 22, no. 1 (1985), pp. 67–78. The documentation is derived from interviews with Mrs. Helen Sanderson conducted by Margaret B. Blackman in 1971, and from interviews with M. (or Emma) Lawrence in 1975 and Robert and Nora Cogo in 1977.

35. Peter Macnair, as cited by Weber in "Photographs as Ethnographic Documents," p. 71.

Tlingit Indians traditionally held ceremonies when a high-ranking person died. Part of the ritual involved a lying-in-state period during which the body was displayed, surrounded by art and other valued possessions. In *The Tlingit Indians,* Aurel Krause quoted a description of a lying-in-state, which he took from a dispatch to the *New York Herald* of April 16, 1881:

> The corpse was ceremonially prepared and placed in a sitting position in the center of the back wall of the house. On his head he wore a wooden hat, carved with figures of the raven, his face was painted, and around his body a woolen blanket decorated with buttons was draped. Two beautiful Chilkat blankets were laid on his knees and on these was a package of letters of recommendation given him by the commanders and other important white people, and a dagger in a carved sheath. To one side of him lay his treasure, mostly woolen blankets packed in several trunks.

After the lying-in-state, if the deceased were not an ixt, the body was cremated. Ashes were stored in small grave houses, along with some of the ceremonial art possessions of the deceased.[36]

Winter and Pond took several images of adults and infants lying in state, which they circulated commercially. Their photographs correlate well with the written descriptions of such scenes. Since it is unlikely that the photographers could have come upon the body unattended, the family of the deceased almost certainly permitted—or even commissioned—them to take the pictures. Winter and Pond's studio was open to the public and it seems likely that Indians would have seen the commercial views of lying-in-state ceremonies and known they were being sold to outsiders. If so, this knowledge did not make Winter and Pond unwelcome at the events.

The lying-in-state practice had actually been witnessed by Europeans long before photography became an option. In the early 1840s, Russian zoologist Ilia Gavrilovich Voznesenskii sketched the funeral ceremony of a Tlingit elder in Sitka. The original is now at the Museum of Anthropology and Ethnography in Leningrad.[37] The arrangement of the body and artwork that Voznesenskii depicts is strikingly similar to the Winter and Pond photographs taken over half a century later. The images show that, despite other changes, these ceremonial practices endured.

Winter and Pond photographed ceremonial art, but they also were interested in the art being made for the tourist market. The sale of art to foreigners started with the first contact with maritime fur traders, who traded for art pieces. Art historian Bill Holm suggests that some fine wooden masks were carved expressly to sell to foreign traders as early as the 1820s. Visitors to Sitka in 1870 saw a variety of "curios" for sale in stores there, and Indians probably were making them for the Russians prior to the political transfer of Alaska to the United States in 1867.[38] In 1881, Commander Henry Glass was pleased to report to the Secretary of the Navy that Indians in Sitka showed

"industry" in making baskets and wood carvings. That same year, missionary Caroline Willard remarked that the Indians "do beautiful work" in several arts, including "weaving from the inner bark of trees baskets, table-mats, hats, etc., which are not only very pretty, but very durable. . . ." She declared, "[A]nd we wish very much to encourage every industry among them, and to develop every talent," and stated that she and her husband planned to design some articles and to give Indians rewards for "designing among themselves." By 1883, missionaries were urging Indian children to make "curiosities" to sell to church societies in the contiguous United States.[39]

After 1887, when steamships began to bring tourists up the Inside Passage, the trade in "curios" escalated. Men made objects such as miniature totem poles, wooden salad forks and spoons with animal figures on the handles, and silver bracelets with totemic designs. Women made a wide variety of basketry items and beadwork.

Many Tlingit and Haida women in southeast Alaska responded actively to Caucasian demand for their artwork. Within their traditional culture, they had developed highly skilled techniques for weaving baskets, mats, capes, hats, and cradle boards for their own use—using spruce root, cedar bark, maidenhair fern, indigenous grasses, and other plant fibers.

36. Krause, *The Tlingit Indians,* pp. 155–56. For more on mortuary customs, see Sergei Kan, "'Wrap Your Father's Brothers in Kind Words': An Analysis of the Nineteenth-Century Tlingit Mortuary and Memorial Rituals" (Ph.D. dissertation, University of Chicago, 1982); Kan, "Memory Eternal: Orthodox Christianity and the Tlingit Mortuary Complex," *Arctic Anthropology,* vol. 24, no. 1 (1987), pp. 32–55; John R. Swanton, "Social Conditions, Beliefs, and Linguistic Relationship of the Tlingit Indians," *Twenty-sixth Annual Report of the Bureau of American Ethnology,* (Washington, D.C., 1908), pp. 391–486; Frederica de Laguna, *Under Mount Saint Elias,* pp. 531–51; Fr. Anatolii Kamenskii, *Tlingit Indians of Alaska* (Fairbanks: University of Alaska Press, 1985), pp. 77–79; and Heinrich Johan Holmberg, *Holmberg's Ethnographic Sketches,* edited by Marvin W. Falk (Fairbanks: University of Alaska Press, 1985).

37. The sketch is reproduced in Thomas Vaughan and Bill Holm, *Soft Gold: The Fur Trade and Cultural Exchange on the Northwest Coast of America* (Portland: Oregon Historical Society, 1982), p. 247. More information on Voznesenskii's research in Alaska can be found in Richard A. Pierce, "Voznesenskii—Scientist in Alaska," *Alaska Journal,* vol. 4, no. 1 (Winter 1975), pp. 11–15.

38. Vaughan and Holm, *Soft Gold,* pp. 96–97. Journal of Sophia Cracroft, 12, 16, and 26 May 1870, in Robert N. De Armond, ed., *Lady Franklin Visits Sitka, Alaska, 1870: The Journal of Sophia Cracroft, Sir John Franklin's Niece* (Anchorage: Alaska Historical Society, 1981), pp. 3, 19, and 54.

39. Commander Glass to Secretary of the Navy, 4 March 1881. "Commanders' Letters 1881 Navy Department," National Archives, Code M 147, Roll 116; Caroline Willard, 29 June 1881, to "My Dear Friends," in McClintock, ed., *Life in Alaska,* p. 39; Julia McNair Wright, *Among the Alaskans* (Philadelphia: Presbyterian Board of Home Missions, 1893), p. 176.

Julia Haley stands behind the counter in her Sitka shop, The Old Russian Trading Post Curio Store.* Below the counter, side-by-side, are a carved and painted bentwood box and a camphorwood chest from China. Although a sign claims the bentwood box was over two hundred years old, it was almost certainly newer. Hanging on the wall are miniature paddles, horn spoons, an octopus bag, carved wooden spoons, halibut hooks, moccasins, and masks. A fine painted spruce root hat hangs on the wall to the right of the counter, near a button blanket that may have been inspired by the Russian double eagle.

* Robert De Armond, pers. comm., 21 July 1987.

When they began weaving for tourists, they made some of these traditional forms, but they also experimented with new designs to appeal to the foreign markets. They covered glass bottles, vases, and canes with weaving; made baskets in the shape of tea kettles, tea cups, and miniature iron cauldrons; copied the shape of communion vessels; and made hats in European style. Some weavers added English lettering to their baskets, using dyed grass in false embroidery.

Women also sewed beadwork designs on cloth from tiny glass beads they purchased from Caucasians. They created items for their own use and to sell back to Caucasians. These beadwork items included pouches, neck ornaments, and moccasins. In the Winter and Pond photographs, beadwork can be seen in the potlatch photographs taken in Klukwan, but also in the photographs of goods offered for sale in the curio stores.

The tourist market provided a significant source of income to some families. While white authorities discouraged the production of ceremonial art for Native use, many government officials, teachers, and missionaries did approve of art that was creately solely as a money-making venture. In 1905, Lieutenant George Emmons, who believed Native art techniques should be taught to Indian children in vocational schools, reported to President Theodore Roosevelt that art was supporting many Indians in Alaska who were "disqualified from more active pursuits through age, sickness, or family circumstances."[40]

In 1905, Winter and Pond wrote, "Excellent carvings in wood, stone, metal, bone and horn can be purchased from the Tlingits. These are not made with any idea of utility beyond a market value, which is decidedly low in comparison with the skill of the carver and the time given to the work." At that time, tourists could buy baskets for about three dollars each, although fancier examples cost more. Within a few years, as baskets became more scarce, prices had doubled. Around 1907, Chilkat blankets for sale started at seventy-five dollars, a substantial sum of money at that time.[41]

Even Indians who did not live on a steamship route took advantage of tourist markets. When E. J. Glave visited the village of Klukwan in 1890, he observed, "Moccasins, fancy bead and leatherwork are hung about and will be sent down to the coast, there to be exchanged to the summer tourists for silver dollars, an element of wealth of which they well know the value."[42] Many of these items can be seen in Winter and Pond's photographs of curio shops in Juneau and Sitka (see p. 38).

The Winter and Pond photographs give an impression of the type of art being made for tourists. Much of this art was very different from the refined ceremonial masterpieces that artists had once made for Native use. It took years of study to master the complex traditional art styles.[43] As young artists entered the white economic system, they could not afford to take time to study art when they could be earning wages. Simultaneously, with pressure from whites, Native cultural contexts for the art were disappearing. Potlatches were becoming more rare, and less and less art was commissioned for use by Indians.

Gradually knowledge of the sophisticated styles declined. The foreigners who had become the primary consumers of Native arts certainly did not require artists to be familiar with the classic northern Northwest Coast Indian formline art styles. Unlike discriminating Native patrons, they expected "crude" art and were willing to buy it. In fact, consumers with no understanding of the abstract formline designs may actually have preferred simpler art.[44] The contrast between the elaborate ceremonial art and the tourist art can be seen vividly in the Winter and Pond images (for example, nos. 20, 74).

There are few known Winter and Pond photographs of artists at work. In the collection are pictures of a woodcarver working on a sculpture, a woman weaving a Chilkat blanket, a Haida woman splitting bark for basket weaving, and several Tlingit women weaving baskets for tourists. Since Winter and Pond were not trying to make an ethnographic study of artists' techniques, they may have felt that arranging to photograph artists was more trouble than it was worth. Yet considering their interest in Indian art, the way the art appealed to tourists, and the variety of shots Winter and Pond customarily took of a given subject, the scarcity of photographs of this nature remains an enigma.

# Interpreting the Images

The Winter and Pond photographs potentially provide several kinds of evidence about experiences of Indians. The physical content of the images vividly depicts the appearance of people, villages, and art in southeast Alaska around the turn of the century. The images also give a basis for hypothesizing about cultural expression and Native-white relations in a time of rapid transition.

40. G. T. Emmons, "A Report on the Conditions and Needs of the Natives of Alaska." 58th Cong., 3rd Sess., 1905, Sen. Ex. Doc. 106, Ser. 4765, p. 2.

41. Winter and Pond, *The Totems of Alaska*; Ella Higginson, *Alaska: The Great Country*, pp. 91–92, 140.

42. Ro Sherman, ed., "The Village of Klukwan, by E. J. Glave of the Frank Leslie's Illustrated Newspaper Expedition to Alaska," in *Alaska Journal*, vol. 4, no. 2 (Spring 1974), pp. 82–87.

43. For a brief discussion of model poles made for tourists in the early part of the twentieth century, see Halpin, *Totem Poles: An Illustrated Guide*, p. 30.

44. Halpin, *Totem Poles: An Illustrated Guide*, p. 30; and Peter Macnair, Alan Hoover, and Kevin Neary, *The Legacy: Tradition and Innovation in Northwest Coast Indian Art* (Vancouver: Douglas & McIntyre; Seattle: University of Washington Press, 1984), p. 191.

*Totem pole models line the street in front of the Nugget Shop, one of the largest curio stores in Juneau.*

It is always wise to be cautious about taking the physical appearance of ethnohistorical photographs at face value. Photographers did have impressions they wanted to project in their images. Nevertheless, while Winter and Pond posed their subjects and recreated scenes in their studio, their pictures seem relatively free of misleading manipulation. Except in a few instances, Winter and Pond's subjects do not appear in anachronistic dress. Their photographs provide much physical evidence of the changes that had taken place in the past decades.

The photographs show the clothes Indians were wearing, the way they incorporated new architectural features into their houses, the totem poles they still displayed, the utensils and tents they used at fishing camps. Although it may not have been their primary purpose, Winter and Pond recorded details that often were not mentioned in written sources. Their images reveal a certain disparity in the conditions in which individual Indians lived. They show Native traditions existing side by side with innovations adopted from foreign contact. The lying-in-state photographs indicate that this mortuary custom persisted into the late nineteenth century in much the same form recorded in Russian accounts and sketches decades earlier. The image of "The Labeler" in the cannery (no. 36) is a lasting reflection of some of the changes Indians experienced as they entered the foreign economic system.

Equally important, the photographs provide the foundation for insight about attitudes—Native attitudes toward their own cultural heritage, and the perspectives of Indians and whites toward each other. Investigating attitudes is always more speculative than studying facts. Factual data can be either corroborated or contradicted; feelings of pride and of ethnic identity are much harder to quantify but no less important. The suggestions the photographs offer about feelings can never be proven, but they contribute notably to understanding.

Diverse seeds of information are embodied in the Winter and Pond photographs. Again and again, the images show Indians displaying elements from their own culture with innovations borrowed from Euro-American settlers. Potlatch dancers wore ceremonial tunics over European suits. Some put on ties, vests, and watch chains, dressing for the occasion in their best European clothes and their best ceremonial items (for example, see nos. 65, 66). Women posed wearing formal button blankets over their dresses (nos. 8, 9). Indians who built new houses in European styles still kept their totem poles before their homes (nos. 48, 49). Some leaders decorated their house fronts with plaques in English that declared the honored status of their Native lineage. Graves were occasionally marked with both Native monuments and Christian-style stone markers (nos. 59, 60). The photographs suggest that when Indians adopted clothes, architectural changes, and new materials for art from the foreigners, they did not reject their heritage.

By their very existence, the photographs also give some indication of relations between Indians and the photographers. Technological restrictions made candid photography impractical; Winter and Pond needed the willing participation of the people they photographed. They received that cooperation from a large number of individuals in contexts ranging from formal studio portraits to dance scenes.

Naturally, the collection that exists today is a record only of Winter and Pond's successful attempts to gain the cooperation of their subjects. It does not reveal their failures. If they were denied permission, or if a subject would not cooperate, the picture did not get taken and no record of the request exists. There are noticeable gaps in the collection. Very few interiors of longhouses are photographed. There are hardly any pictures of Indians at work in white industries. Winter and Pond did not photograph specific dances, although they did obtain posed images at real potlatches. They rarely photographed artists making art objects. Since interior views often required flash powder or flash bombs that were messy and not entirely safe, and "action" photographs required subjects to freeze their motion, the photographers may have omitted such images because of the limitations of their technology.

By revealing what Winter and Pond thought their white audiences would want to buy, the collection stimulates ideas about white attitudes toward Indians. One might expect the photographers to have concentrated on images that downplayed evidence of assimilation—of European influence—yet this was not always the case. Their audiences accepted photographs showing the ways contemporary Indians lived. The images suggest animation and personality. Still, recording personal names did not seem important to Winter and Pond: they did not try to rescue their subjects from anonymity.

The Winter and Pond photographs are valuable because of what they reflect about people's lives in a time of change. They include a remarkable range of images, from studio portraits to village scenes to photographs of dancers at potlatches. They provide physical evidence that makes suggestions about attitudes. The very existence of the photographs reveals that in a variety of situations Indians chose to cooperate with Winter and Pond, or at least to tolerate their presence. Perhaps most important, the photographs bring the individuals to life. In preserving a record of these strong survivors of tumultuous change, the photographs enhance our understanding of the experiences of Alaskans around the turn of the century.

*Interior of Winter and Pond's portrait studio.*

# Portraits

Styk Indian Dancers,Alaska.

## 1. "Styk Indian Dancers, Alaska"

Two Indians with painted faces and nose rings pose in dance tunics with elaborately beaded cuffs and neck ornaments. They both wear octopus bags, a type of Athabascan beaded pouch that was popular among Athabascan and Tlingit Indians as part of ceremonial regalia.* While Winter and Pond labeled the photograph "Styk Indians," it is more likely of Tlingit Indians dressed in Athabascan costumes. The style of beadwork is Tlingit, and it was probably developed from the neighboring Athabascans.† Such ceremonial garb was reportedly very expensive and highly prized.

Guns frequently appear in historical photographs of dance outfits. The lines of the guns form a point almost in the center of the photograph, reflecting the photographers' interest in symmetry. 87–288

* See Kaplan and Barsness, *Raven's Journey*, p. 170.

† Bill Holm, pers. comm., June 1988.

## 2. "Indian Dancers, Alaska"

At right Winter and Pond tried to overcome the limitations of a still photograph by evoking a sense of drama. As in the facing photograph (no. 1), the guns form a large V in the center of the photograph. In both of these images, Winter and Pond relied on the patience and cooperation of their subjects, having them pose at stiff attention for the duration of the exposure. 87–287

184    Indian Dancers, Alaska.                    Winter & Pond. Photo.

Saginaw Jake, of Killisnoo, Alaska.    Winter & Pond, Ph

### 3. "Saginaw Jake of Killisnoo, Alaska"

Saginaw Jake (left), also known as Killisnoo Jake, a leader from the village of Killisnoo, poses in his Native policeman's uniform and badge. Some such uniforms were adapted from clothing obtained from naval officers. The photographers posed Saginaw Jake standing with his hand on a tree section, echoing the conventions of portraiture common at the time. This is one of the few photographs for which Winter and Pond identified their subject by name. Saginaw Jake appears in front of his house in the photograph on p. 32. 87–227

### 4. "Chilkat Indian and Blanket, Alaska"

Tlingit and Haida dance clothing was made to be seen in action. This man wears a Chilkat ceremonial dancing blanket, a highly prized dance article made from mountain goat wool and cedar bark, using complex weaving techniques.* He poses as if in the midst of a dance turn, holding one arm extended to display the full sweep of the blanket. While the photographers wanted to show the blanket in use, it is unlikely that they intended to document a specific dance. Although they usually chose painted backdrops in studio images, here they selected a neutral screen to avoid competing with the striking design of the blanket. A tree section, used as a prop, has been covered with a fur. 87–039

* These remarkable weaving techniques are described in Cheryl Samuel, *The Chilkat Dancing Blanket* (Seattle: Pacific Search Press, 1982).

185    Chilkat Indian and Blanket, Alaska.    Winter & Pond, Photo

## 5. [Young Women in Studio]

Here Winter and Pond made no effort to hide the artificiality of the studio setting. These women are posed symmetrically in front of a painted window scene. The fur capes, made from skins sewn together, were a Native form of dress, but were being abandoned by 1881 when Aurel Krause reported that fur capes were "being crowded out by the woolen blanket."* Fur robes such as these appear in several Winter and Pond pictures, and it is possible that the photographers provided them without seeking to conceal the modern dresses or the headscarves. However, ground squirrel or marmot blankets still exist in Indian ownership in Alaska today.† 87–075

* Krause, *The Tlingit Indians*, p. 101.

† Bill Holm, pers. comm., June 1988.

## 6. "Native Women, Juneau, Alaska"

Two Tlingit women pose outdoors in Juneau. Again, their furs were probably provided by Winter and Pond. While Indian women often wore wool blankets over their dresses, furs such as these were reportedly prized in the home as warm afghans. 87–074

Native Women, Juneau, Alaska.

### 7. [Man with Wool Blanket]

This man wears a wool trade blanket. In the 1880s, wool blankets were widely used as currency; in the Chilkat region at that time, they were worth three to four dollars each. 87–231

### 8. "Wife of Chilcat Chief, Alaska"

Winter and Pond's studio was visited by Indian acquaintances from the Chilkat region who passed through Juneau. This woman sits for her portrait wearing a ceremonial button blanket clasped with a safety pin over her dress. In labeling this picture "Wife of Chilcat Chief," the photographers suggest that their white audiences would be interested in her status, but not in her name. Button blankets worn by women were decorated with rows of commercial shell buttons, and often had a wide border of red cloth attached to a darker wool blanket.* The earliest blankets had buttons only along the border; designs later became more elaborate. 87–042

* De Laguna, *Under Mount Saint Elias*, p. 442.

Wife of Chilcat Chief, Alaska.

## 9. [Man and Woman in Dance Costume]

A couple poses in Winter and Pond's Juneau studio. The woman wears a Hudson's Bay Company wool trade blanket, transformed into a ceremonial robe by the embellishment of buttons. She chose an elegant dress for this portrait. The man stands in similarly prized regalia, a woven Chilkat tunic. This tunic is discussed and illustrated in *The Chilkat Blanket* by George Emmons, with notes on the blanket designs by Franz Boas.*

The man's unkempt headgear may represent a type of hat that originated with a legend about how Raven made a hat by placing kelp in the middle of a jellyfish. Originally flicker feathers were used for the hat, but they were replaced by feather dusters.[†] 87–041

* Emmons, *The Chilkat Blanket* (American Museum of Natural History, 1907), pp. 397–98.

[†] See Maureen Milburn, "Louis Shotridge and the Objects of Everlasting Esteem," in Kaplan and Barsness, *Raven's Journey*, p. 71.

## 10. [Yeilgooxu and Coudahwot]

In 1895 in Klukwan, Winter and Pond photographed the same dance tunic that appears in the photograph at left (no. 9). At far right it is worn by a different man—Yeilgooxu, or George Shotridge, the hereditary caretaker of the Whale House there (see nos. 64, 71, 72). He has a nose ring and a painted face and holds a raven rattle. The man beside him, Coudahwot, wears a leather painted tunic and a ceremonial clan hat displaying his crest.* Coudahwot's tunic is now in the University Museum, University of Pennsylvania. The leggings both men wear show the influence of Athabascan artists, who embroidered flattened porcupine quills into geometric patterns and introduced this technique to the nearby Tlingits.[†] 87–296

* Milburn, "Louis Shotridge and the Objects of Everlasting Esteem," pp. 60–61; Bill Holm and Bill Reid, *Form and Freedom* (Houston: Institute for the Arts, Rice University, 1975), p. 18.

[†] Kaplan and Barsness, *Raven's Journey*, p. 186.

Native Boy. Juneau, Alaska.          Winter & Pond, Photo.

### 11. "Native Boy, Juneau, Alaska"

This young boy wears nothing that relates to his Indian background. As usual, the photographers took care with this pose, having the boy extend one leg slightly in front of the other, possibly on tiptoes, and rest his hand on a section of a tree. 87–067

### 12. "Native Boys, Juneau, Alaska"

Winter and Pond labeled the image at right "Native Boys," but made no other obvious effort to emphasize the children's Indian heritage. The boys sit in a carefully constructed pyramid, against a painted backdrop, and those in the first row place their hands in similar positions. 87–072

230 NATIVE BOYS, JUNEAU, ALASKA     WINTER & POND PHOTO.

230    Native Boys, Juneau, Alaska.                    Winter & Pond, Photo.

### 13. [Woman by Fence]

This woman wears an elegant dress, and poses with her arm on a fence. The portrait may have been commissioned by the subject's family, rather than taken for commercial circulation, as it has no caption and resembles private poses of Caucasian women. 87–198

### 14. [Two Women in Studio]

The portrait at right was probably taken at a private sitting; very few of Winter and Pond's photographs of Indians in formal, modern-style clothing were produced for sale. The woman on the left wears a wedding ring. Smallpox vaccinations had been introduced, and the young girl, possibly her daughter, has a vaccination scar on her left arm. 87–289

## 15. [Man in House]

The image appears to have been taken in a house. In the background is a framed painting and fancy wallpaper. The man poses in a double-breasted suit and a tie, holding a metal-headed cane. His cap bears the insignia "Takou Chief." A brass cast eagle and two miniature American flags add a patriotic air to the composition. At the same time, the man stands before three Chilkat ceremonial dancing blankets, and a well-preserved, carved and painted frontlet rests behind his left shoulder. The photograph includes art and symbols of prestige from the Native culture and the foreign culture. Winter and Pond later obtained a lying-in-state portrait of this man, wearing the frontlet (no. 79). 87–204

## 16. [Woman with Child]

This woman wears a formal, fitted dress and a delicate fringed shawl; the child by her side strikes a figure in similarly impressive clothing. Both stand before a Chilkat dancing blanket, an elegant art object from their own culture. This blanket appears to be the same one that is seen to the left of the man in the facing photograph (no. 15), and the woman may be his wife. 87–297

249  NATIVE CHILDREN JUNEAU, ALASKA                    WINTER & POND  PHOTO.

### 17. "Native Children, Juneau Alaska"

Six Indian children appear to sit in front of a building in Juneau, but actually the boards were set up in Winter and Pond's studio. The rough animal design etched on the wall behind them is based loosely on Tlingit art traditions. While two of the children have blankets, no effort was made to hide the European-style street clothes they all wear. 87–071

### 18. "Native Girls, Juneau, Alaska"

Winter and Pond also took this image in their studio, using the same constructed background seen in the preceding photograph (no. 17). The photograph conveys spontaneity, with the door just cracked ajar, but actually it is carefully posed, with one girl's hand resting lightly on the lap of her friend. A carved wooden salmon hanging on the wall suggests the Native background of the subjects. 87–070

245 Native Girls, Juneau, Alaska. Winter & Pond, Photo.

Native Girl, Juneau, Alaska.    Winter & Pond, Photo.

## 19. "Native Girl, Juneau, Alaska"

Winter and Pond had this young woman stand
on a grass floor covering and lean against a tree
section, creating the impression of the outdoors
inside the studio. 87–203

## 20. "Native Women Selling Curios, Sitka, Alaska"

Although they labeled the photograph, "Sitka,"
Winter and Pond posed the curio sellers at right in
their studio, bringing in a false door to give the
appearance of the outdoors. The wares on display
may have come out of Winter and Pond's curio shop,
and resemble the items tourists would find for sale
along the docks. Baskets, silver bracelets, and small
wooden models such as the canoe were all fairly
common. The carved wooden salad spoons and
forks were a form of art developed for the tourist
trade, and many examples were brought East by
tourists. To the left of the women is a beautifully
carved wood dance staff, and an engraved halibut
hook hangs on the boards above them. Their fur
robes may have been provided by Winter and Pond;
most other historical photographs of women selling
curios show only blankets over their dresses. 87–294

## 21. [Women Posing as Curio Sellers]

Tourists who cruised the Inside Passage on summer steamship excursions were met at each dock by Indian women selling arts made for the tourist trade. Winter and Pond recreated this marketplace in their studio, perhaps assuming that tourists would be interested in a record of a scene they had witnessed. The baskets, nose rings, and wooden and horn spoons on the mat may actually have come from Winter and Pond's curio shop. The wares are scattered in front of the women, but there is nothing haphazard about the composition of the photograph. The women are seated so that their outer garments alternate between blankets and furs. Seeking symmetry, the photographers placed a large basket directly between the two center figures. 87–313

## 22. [Women Wearing Nose Rings and Posing as Curio Sellers]

Some of the nose rings displayed in the facing photograph (no. 21) are being worn by the women here. This old custom of adornment had essentially disappeared by the turn of the century, but photographs of Indians in ceremonial regalia sometimes show nose rings in place (see, for example, no. 10). Made of indigenous copper in precontact times, the rings were fashioned from commercial silver when it became available through trade.* 87–314

* De Laguna, *Under Mount Saint Elias*, p. 445.

Wrangell Medicine Man.

### 23. "Wrangell Medicine Man"

A shaman, or spiritual leader, was known in Tlingit as "*ixt.*" This man wears a wig simulating the uncut hair of an ixt, and an apron decorated with puffin beaks and dentalia. Ixts often posed with rattles, but this man displays a rare carving of a bird with moveable wings operated by strings.* This carving is now in the Burke Museum at the University of Washington. It was collected as part of an ixt's accoutrements. Winter and Pond did not feel that the man's everyday shirt, evidence of foreign contact, would deter tourists from purchasing the image. 87–250

\* For a more detailed discussion of Tlingit shamanic rattles, see Aldona Jonaitis, *Art of the Northern Tlingit* (Seattle: University of Washington Press, 1986).

### 24. [Man with Necklace]

Winter and Pond took several poses of this man, whom they called "Takou Indian Doctor." At right, he wears a necklace symbolizing his high position. Puffin beaks decorate the fringe of his blanket. 87–248

### 25. "Chilkat Indian/Doctor"

This is a portrait of Skundoo, a well-known ixt from the Chilkat village of Kokwoltoo, but in this image, only the caption identifies his role. Skundoo, whose Tlingit name was Scxaan du oo, was a member of the Thunderbird clan. According to oral tradition he had the power to see right through people. 87–038

### 26. "Indian Medicine Man"

Usually Winter and Pond's photographic subjects wore modern clothing. This photograph of Skundoo pretending to practice his healing is an exception; he poses with a rattle in each hand and wears only a leather apron with coins attached to its fringe. The photograph is copyrighted 1894. Around the time it was taken, Skundoo was tried in the district court in Juneau for responsibility in the death of a Native woman. He had identified her as a witch, and when she refused to confess, she had been forced to starve. Skundoo was sentenced to three years at San Quentin. The action was intended by Caucasian authorities to discourage other ixts, and did cause some to abandon their work voluntarily. When Skundoo returned from prison, he gave reenactments of ixt activities to support himself.* 87–258

* *Alaska Searchlight* (Juneau), vol. 1, no. 19 (22 April 1895), pp. 1–2; Frederica de Laguna, pers. comm., 25 September 1987.

TAKOU INDIAN DOCTOR.

WPC

254 TAKOU INDIAN, DOCTOR, ALASKA     COPYRIGHT BY WINTER & POND.

### 27. "Takou Indian Doctor, Alaska"

This image was probably taken inside Winter and Pond's studio, with a background designed to look like an exterior wall. Ixts wore their hair long and were thought to lose their powers if their hair was cut; some whites combatted shamans by cutting their hair. Nevertheless, as late as 1909, Rev. A. J. Whipkey, a missionary in Hoonah, complained that ixts still practiced there.* 87–215

* Whipkey, "Last Winter at Hoonah," *Assembly Herald.*

### 28. [Baby in Sling]

This photograph is probably Winter and Pond's most successful attempt to capitalize on the image of the cute Indian baby. The infant wears a cap trimmed in buttons, and snuggles in a bark sling that is rigged to a rocking mechanism. The swinging of the sling was reportedly supposed to remind the baby of the motion in the womb. The baby's button cap is Tlingit in style, but the moccasins and birchbark sling are probably Athabascan. Winter and Pond also produced this image as a Christmas card. 87–180

In this view of a family from the Tlingit village of Kake, the mother holds a baby on her lap and smiles at the camera. The clothes are almost certainly those of daily use: for the woman and girls, loose dresses and head kerchiefs; the boys wear shirts and trousers; and the man, a vest and high rubber boots. Nothing in this photograph emphasizes the ethnic background of the Indians, but Winter and Pond clearly felt it would appeal to tourists. Perhaps this is because it presents a family complete with a happy family dog—a picture that would strike a resonance in people from any culture. 87–087

## 30. [Post Office, Chilkat]

Solomon Ripinsky, an immigrant from Poland, came to the Chilkat area in 1886 as a school teacher. He later became a merchant and fur trader who served as postmaster.* Standing to the right of center in a white tie and a prominent moustache, he poses here shortly after the opening of the post office. A group of Indians sits at the right edge of the picture. One Indian woman wears a fancy hat for the photograph. With the exception of the women's head kerchiefs, the Indians' clothing differs very little from that of the whites. 87–1565

* Robert De Armond, pers. comm., 23 May 1988.

57.
Indian Children.

## 31. "Indian Children"

Indian children pose for Winter and Pond at a camp along a beach. A stovepipe protrudes from the canvas tent. 87–326

## 32. [Two Women with Cat]

These two women appear in skirts and blouses and the head kerchief often worn by Alaskan Indian women around the turn of the century. Although they do not appear to be wealthy, they both wear lip pegs in their lower lip—a sign of prestige.* Traditionally, high-ranking Tlingit women wore large elliptical labrets, some of them two inches long. By the late nineteenth century, labrets of this size were not common, but some women wore smaller pegs such as those seen here.[†] 87–303

* This discrepancy was pointed out by a Native consultant, 18 Aug. 1987.

† Krause, *The Tlingit Indians*, p. 96–200; Albert P. Niblack, *The Coast Indians of Southern Alaska and Northern British Columbia* (New York: Johnson Reprint Corporation, 1970), plate XI, pp. 266–67.

215 OLD THLINGIT WOMEN, FORT WRANGEL, ALASKA
COPYRIGHT BY WINTER & POND.

### 33. [Woman in Dance Regalia]

In dance costume, the woman at left poses in front of a button blanket. Since Indians did not bring full collections of art to the studio, Winter and Pond went to the field to take photographs of art in use. The woman holds a white feather duster ornament and wears a hat made from a portion of a Chilkat blanket.  87–201

### 34. "Fort Wrangel Indian in Dancing Costume, Alaska"

This man poses against the same background seen in the facing photograph (no. 33), holding an elegantly carved dance staff. His tunic sports a frog crest in appliqué, outlined by large and small buttons. His unusual clan hat appears to have a hanging fringe, possibly of dentalia. It resembles more circular hats that reflect Russian influence. 87–205

Fort Wrangel Indian in Dancing Costume, Alaska.    Winter & Pond, Photo.

Tlingit Indians, Wrangel, Alaska. Copyright 1896 by Winter & Pond

## 35. "Tlingit Indians, Wrangel, Alaska"

This photograph was copyrighted in 1896. While Winter and Pond identified the site as Wrangell, it has also sometimes been called a portrait of Chief Kowee of Juneau.* In either case, the women may have been wives of the man. At that time there were still instances of polygyny—multiple wives—among the Indians, although government officials and missionaries had already started an active campaign to eradicate the practice. The subjects display prestigious clothing: the man wears a uniform, while the women wear button blankets over their commercial dresses. 87–141

* This discrepancy in identification is noted in the finder's aid to PCA 87 (Winter and Pond Collection). Wrangell was also formerly spelled Wrangel; the captions on the Winter and Pond negatives are inconsistent. Wrangell is the modern usage.

## 36. " 'The Labeler,' Sitkof Bay Cannery, Alaska"

An Indian woman works inside a cannery putting labels on salmon cans. Canneries were a source of income for both men and women, and many families moved in the summers to be near canneries. Few photographers took pictures of Indians working in canneries, perhaps because they thought these views would not be of interest to white audiences. The Sitkof Brand of pink salmon was packed by the Chatham Cannery, which operated in Sitkoh Bay from 1902 to 1965. The Sitkof Brand label was used between 1907 and 1928.* 87–190

* Patricia Roppel, pers. comm., 23 August 1987; Robert N. De Armond, pers. comm., 23 May 1988.

311 CAMP OF AUK INDIANS, ALASKA
COPYRIGHT BY WINTER & POND.

311      Camp of Auk Indians, Alaska.
Copyright 1896 by Winter & Pond

Camp of Auk Indians, Alaska.

261  Camp of Auk Indians, Alaska.  Copyright 1895 by Winter & Pond.

## 37. "Camp of Auk Indians, Alaska"

A family of Auk Indians, at left, works at a temporary summer fishing camp. The backbone of a filleted halibut hangs on the line between the tents to dry. According to a Native consultant, the meat left on the backbone will be boiled when half dried. The goods scattered around the camp show a mixture of Native-manufactured items and objects purchased in stores. A ladle made of mountain sheep horn appears in the foreground, showing that Indians still used them in utilitarian ways. The handwoven baskets here are much larger than the small baskets women made to sell to tourists. Some of the wooden containers are bentwood boxes made by Native craftsmen by steaming and bending a single board. Among other uses, they carried seal oil. Also in view are iron pails and commercial wooden crates. A woman works over a large metal tub. She may have been extracting fish oil to use on berries and dried halibut, although formerly this was a larger operation than the photograph depicts. The photograph was copyrighted in 1896. 87–079

## 38. "Camp of Auk Indians, Alaska"

Indians at the summer fishing camp interrupt their work to pose for Winter and Pond. The iron cauldron steaming on the right probably contains fish oil. The young boy holds up a spruce root basket, probably used here either for berries or to carry water. These are rare photographs. Photographers did not frequently travel to these camps, which were off the regular steamship routes. They are important pictures today because they depict scenes that were part of the annual summer experiences of many southeast Alaskan Indians. The photograph was copyrighted in 1895. 87–080

### 39. "Indian Laundry, Juneau, Alaska"

In addition to making arts and crafts, Indian women earned money by performing domestic services. This couple sits in front of a tidy house in Juneau below a sign that advertises "Washing Woman." The date on the sign appears to be Feb. 8, 1890. 87–066

Indian Canoe Race - Juneau, Alaska.

### 40. "Indian Canoe Race, Juneau, Alaska"

On the Fourth of July, Indians raced old-style canoes across the channel to Douglas Island and back. Taku and Auk Indians competed, and sometimes teams came from farther afield for the event. Some years as many as eight canoes raced for cash prizes.* 87–065

* Robert De Armond, pers. comm., 12 July 1987.

# Villages

## 41, 42. [Chilkat Village]

Probably taken in the spring of 1895, these two views show the Tlingit village of Klukwan on the Chilkat River, some thirty miles from Lynn Canal in the northern part of the Alaskan panhandle. They depict a village in the midst of change. Houses are still in the traditional style of the communal longhouse, facing out toward the water. Some are made with rough boards, lack windows, and have open doorways. Others are painted, appear to have been built from milled boards, and have windows and hinged doors. Most of the houses with windows are large and were probably owned by high-ranking families that were wealthy enough to make the renovations. Canoes line the beach, some covered with blankets and tarps to protect them from cracking in the sun. The cottonwood canoe in the foreground of photograph 41 is probably the one Winter and Pond used the day the picture was taken. The wooden racks in front of the houses were used for hanging nets,

fish, and other items for drying. Early in the 1880s, Presbyterian missionaries came to the Chilkat region and urged Indians to adopt Christian burial practices, but some Native grave houses are still seen in the distance. Although Klukwan, the largest of the Chilkat villages, had a population between 500 and 600 in the 1880s, by the time these images were taken the population had decreased to about 320.* 87001, 87–002

* Missionaries' efforts to change burial practices—and the difficulties these missionaries encountered—are described by Caroline Willard in McClintock, *Life in Alaska*. For population trends, see Russell Sackett, *The Chilkat Tlingit: A General Overview* (University of Alaska, Occasional Paper No. 23, November 1979), p. 29.

881 KLIN-QUAN, INDIAN VILLAGE ALASKA
COPYRIGHT BY WINTER & POND.

## 43. "Klin-quan, Indian Village, Alaska"

Canoes line the beach of the old Haida village of Klinquan in this image, probably taken around 1897. All the houses have had windows added, but the interiors are almost certainly still communal. The central smoke holes are very evident. In 1898, James Millar, a white man living in Klinquan, wrote, "Eight years ago it was almost deserted . . . but now their are quite a population [sic]. . . . [A]bout twenty five families live here most of the time and about 50 or 60 children." He explained that a cannery and fishery near the village hired all the Indians who wanted to work, and Indians were returning to the site. He concluded, "So owing to these industries, the Village is growing very rapidly."* 87–090

* James Millar to Governor John Green Brady, 21 April 1898, in Brady Papers, The Beinecke Rare Book and Manuscript Library, Yale University.

## 44. "Auk Village, Juneau, Alaska"

Auk Indians, a branch of the Tlingit, originally made their home about sixteen miles northwest of Juneau. Many moved to the new gold rush town of Juneau in the early 1880s, where they could earn up to two dollars a day working for miners as diggers, packers, and woodcutters.* In a departure from tradition, they used pilings to raise the beachfront houses from the water, and faced them away from the water. A second row of houses, built as the village expanded, is barely visible behind the first. All houses used milled lumber. By the time this image was taken, about 1910, wood stoves had replaced the central fire pits. 87–1328

* Krause, *The Tlingit Indians*, p. 68.

COPYRIGHT BY WINTER & POND.

### 45. "Indian Visitors Attending Potlatch at Kok-wol-too Village, Alaska"

In this image, copyrighted in 1895, Indians crowd in canoes at the northern Tlingit village Kok-wol-too, on the north bank of the Chilkat River. Men wear derby hats. The large central house is painted and has a new front with windows and a door; an American flag is displayed for the occasion. Some of the structures along the beach may be storage sheds or smokehouses rather than dwellings. This scene, apparently taken in summer, shows little dance regalia; despite Winter and Pond's caption, Native informants suggest that it may have been a gathering other than a winter potlatch. The village had a population of about seventy in 1890. Shortly after this photograph was taken, a mud slide buried the village and it was abandoned.* 87–048

* Sackett, *The Chilkat Tlingit*, p. 51.

## 46. [Canoes by Yindastuki]

Early in 1895, men launch canoes in front of the Tlingit village of Yin-day-stuck-e-yah, or Yindastuki, at
the mouth of the Chilkat River. Sails help propel the canoe. Smokehouses are on the river bank, with
community houses in the background. Like those in the other villages in the Chilkat region, some houses
have windows and doors and some do not. The square frame on the left may be a house under construction.
The name Yindastuki meant "where everything from afar drifts on shore." It was traditionally a gathering
site for meetings between villages. In 1890, there was a population of about 143.* 87–046

* Sackett, *The Chilkat Tlingit*, pp. 32–34.

INDIAN VILLAGE, HOWKAN, ALASKA

## 47. "Indian Village, Howkan, Alaska"

Howkan, a Haida village on Long Island near Prince
of Wales Island, was photographed by Winter and
Pond in about 1897. Totem poles still stand before
the longhouses, and canoes line the beach. All of
the houses pictured have had windows added to
their fronts, and some have been painted or whitewashed. The figure on the top of the totem pole
in the center is a double-finned killer whale. Flag
poles like the one on the left are frequently seen in
village scenes from this time period. 87–050

## 48. [Howkan]

At right Howkan is shown from another angle, with the double-finned killer whale toward
the right of the photograph. The architecture of some of the houses differs from that of the
traditional Native longhouse. The large white house on the left is the most dramatic
departure from tradition, but a totem pole still stands in front of it in accordance with
custom. The house belonged to Moses Kulthgid, and social events were held in the second
story. To its right is a smaller house of modern style, with a stone monument in the front
yard, showing the influence of missionaries. After a mortuary potlatch was given for the
deceased, the stone would be moved to the grave.* In the background behind this house is
a Presbyterian church or school. 87–091

* Margaret B. Blackman, pers. comm., 12 Sept. 1987 and 21 March 1988.

Totem Poles, Chief Kat-a-shan's House, Fort Wrangel, Alaska    Winter & Pond, Photo.

### 49. [Kadishan's House]

Kadishan (or Katashan), a leader in Wrangell, built this house (left) in 1887. Winter and Pond reported that his ancestors were high-ranking Haidas who intermarried with the Tlingits and moved to the Stikine River region. The poles are considerably older than the large house. Although he adopted new architecture, Kadishan still faced his house toward the beach and preserved his poles by supporting them with a prop. His neighbor's house is in the traditional longhouse style, although it has a fence, windows, a door, and a flag pole in front. 87–123

### 50. "Totem Poles, Chief Kat-a-shan's House, Fort Wrangel, Alaska"

Seen from the beach, Kadishan's house presents an imposing image with the two totem poles before it. The houses on either side are the traditional shape of Tlingit homes, although both use milled lumber. This photograph was probably taken some years earlier than the facing photograph (no. 49), as the poles show less deterioration. 87–120

CHIEF KAHL-TEEN'S TOTEM POLE, LE, ALASKA    COPYRIGHT BY WINTER & POND.

## 51. "Chief Kahl-Teen's Totem Pole, Fort Wrangle, Alaska"

This totem pole, new when the picture was taken, was erected in the memory of Kahl-teen, a leader in Wrangell. In *The Totems of Alaska*, Winter and Pond wrote, "The workmanship is of a higher order than that of the older carvings, which is probably due to the fact that modern tools were used in the execution of the work. The use of paint artistically applied adds to the attractive appearance of the totem." The top figure represents a mountain or rock. It is unusual for geographical features to appear on poles; when such features do appear as crests, they often indicate right to control the territory.* The second figure on the pole, a frog, greatly resembles the crest on the tunic in photograph number 34. A replica has recently been carved in Wrangell by contemporary artists Steve Brown and Wayne Price. 87–128

* Steve Brown, pers. comm., 27 July 1987; De Laguna, *Under Mount Saint Elias*, p. 456. De Laguna suggests that the use of mountains as crests may have been adopted from the Athabascans, who commonly identified communities with mountains.

## 52. "Chief Shake's [Shakes's] Totem, Fort Wrangle, Alaska"

The pole at right belonged to Chief Shakes, a prominent leader of the Nan-yan-yi clan in Wrangell. According to Winter and Pond, it was carved by Toh-yot, and was commissioned by Chief Shakes in honor of his wife, who was a daughter of Chief Kadishan. Another source, however, states that it was raised in 1896 in honor of two of Chief Shakes's sons.* A replica carved by contemporary artists Steve Brown and Wayne Price was raised in Wrangell on the second of July 1987. 87–126

* Winter and Pond, *The Totems of Alaska*, p. 6; Keithahn, *Monuments in Cedar*, p. 91.

CHIEF
SHAKE'S
TOTEM.

© WPC

688 CHIEF SHAKE'S TO EM, FORT WRANGLE, ALASKA COPYRIGHT BY WINTER & POND

CHIEF SHAKE'S TOTEMS, FORT WRANGLE, ALASKA    COPYRIGHT BY WINTER & POND.

### 53. "Chief Shake's [Shakes's] Totems, Fort Wrangle, Alaska"

These mortuary poles stood in front of the house of Shakes in Wrangell. The pole on the left represents Gonakadet, a sea monster, while the pole on the right represents a grizzly bear, perhaps the supernatural bear who led the Nan-yan-yi people up a mountain to safety in legendary times. The ashes of Shakes VI's father and mother were placed in the Gonakadet pole, and ashes of his brother were held in the grizzly bear pole. Replicas of these poles stand on Shakes Island in Wrangell today in front of a rebuilt version of Shakes's original house.* 87–115

* Edward L. Keithahn, "The Authentic History of Shakes Island and Clan" (Wrangell Historical Society, 1981), pp. 1, 2; Keithahn, *Monuments in Cedar: The Authentic Story of the Totem Pole* (New York: Bonanza Books, 1963), pp. 54–55.

### 54. "Totem Poles, Chief Shake's House, Fort Wrangel, Alaska"

Children stand in front of Chief Shakes's house in Wrangell (right), holding ceremonial art objects for the camera. Two boys present clan hats. A patchwork quilt has been spread on the porch, for display as well as to protect the art objects resting on it. These quilts reportedly became popular among Indians in southeast Alaska when Natives learned from missionaries how to make them. 87–117

COPYRIGHT BY WINTER & POND.

Shake's House, Fort Wrangell, Alaska.

## 55. "Indian Totem Poles, Kake, Alaska"

These painted totem poles at the Tlingit village of Kake were probably fairly new when Winter and Pond photographed them around 1894. Traditionally, Tlingit Indians in southeast Alaska practiced a code of justice that demanded retribution for wrongdoing. In *The Totems of Alaska*, Winter and Pond noted that the top figure of the large pole in this picture is a white man. Stating that the pole was erected over the grave of a Kake victim, they explained: "The totem reminds the members of the Raven clan that the life of a white man must be forfeited." Whether or not this is true, the story enhanced the interest of the image in the eyes of tourists. Totem poles in Kake were burned in 1913, possibly by villagers who had come under the influence of missionaries.* 87–84A

* George E. Beck to Edward Keithahn, quoted in Keithahn, *Monuments in Cedar*, pp. 85–87.

E38  Totems at Indian River. SITKA. ALASKA.

WINTER·POND·
PHOTO.

## 56. "Totems at Indian River, Sitka, Alaska"

Governor John Green Brady, a former Presbyterian missionary who served as Alaska's governor from 1897 to 1906, asked Tlingit and Haida Indians to donate totem poles to be preserved in a park in Sitka. Sonihat, a leading man in the Haida village of Kasaan, was the first to respond to his request, donating this pole and interior house posts in 1901. Brady exhibited the fifty-foot pole at the St. Louis Exposition of 1904 and at the Lewis and Clark Exposition in Portland in 1905, before establishing it in its permanent home in Sitka. A replica stands in the Sitka National Historical Park there today.* 87–094

* Victoria Wyatt, "A Unique Attraction: The Alaskan Totem Poles at St. Louis Exposition of 1904," in Terrence Cole, ed., *The Alaska Journal: A 1986 Collection,* pp. 14–23 (Anchorage: Alaska Northwest Publishing Company, 1986); Susan F. Edelstein, ed., *Carved History: The Totem Poles and House Posts of Sitka National Historical Park* (Anchorage: Alaska Natural History Association, 1980), unpaged. Information on Governor Brady and his collecting activities can also be found in Cole, *Captured Heritage,* pp. 202–5, and in Hinckley, *Alaskan John G. Brady: Missionary, Businessman, Judge, and Governor.* Ted Hinckley discusses the interest of Presbyterian missionaries in preserving Native arts in "Sheldon Jackson as Preserver of Alaska's Native Culture," *Pacific Historical Review,* vol. 33 (Nov. 1964), pp. 411–24.

195        Indian Graves, Chilkat, Alaska.        Copyright 1895 by Winter & Pond.

## 57. "Indian Graves, Chilkat, Alaska"

The grave houses at left, behind the village of Klukwan, probably held the remains of high-ranking Tlingit Indians. Some grave houses were decorated with crest designs. Traditionally, ashes of cremated bodies were placed in grave houses, along with some of the belongings of the deceased. By the time this photograph was taken, some uncremated bodies were deposited in grave houses in coffins.* According to a sketch in Krause's *The Tlingit Indians* (p. 160), the two houses right of center were standing in 1881. Even that early, the house with the boarded front had a window, and flag poles were present. The white picket fences in the background probably surround other graves. When Tlingit Indians began burying their dead in Christian fashion, they sometimes adopted the Caucasian practice of enclosing the burial sites in picket fences. The white paint was reported to be a commercial introduction, and may have been whitewash. The photograph was copyrighted in 1895. 87–025

* Bill Holm, pers. comm., June 1988.

## 58. "Chilkat Frog Grave House"

This closer view of a grave house in the facing photograph (no. 57) shows the frog decoration, a crest belonging to the person it honors. Abalone shell decorates the eyes, and once filled the mouth. The frog has probably been repainted.* This same crest design appears on the wool tunic worn by a dancer in photograph number 66. 87–028

* Steve Brown, pers. comm., 27 July 1987, Juneau.

INDIAN TOTEMS & GRAVES, FORT WRANGLE, ALASKA COPYRIGHT BY WINTER & POND.

### 59. "Indian Totems and Graves, Fort Wrangle, Alaska"

In the late nineteenth century, Indians in many parts of southeast Alaska began using stone grave markers at the urging of Christian missionaries. These did not always replace Native memorial poles. Shakes VII of Wrangell erected this memorial pole, known as the "One-legged fisherman pole," to honor his uncle, Kauk-ish, who died in 1897.[*] He also put up a stone marker with the engraving, "In memory of Kauk-ish, died 1897, age 68 yrs." The fencing of graves, which Indians may have first adopted from Russians, had become fairly common in southern parts of the archipelago by the 1880s.[†] 87–134

[*] Keithahn, *Monuments in Cedar*, p. 147. This pole is discussed by Steve Brown in "From Taquan to Klukwan: Tracing the Work of an Early Tlingit Master Artist," in Corey, ed., *Faces, Voices and Dreams*, pp. 157–75.

[†] Niblack, *The Coast Indians*, pp. 356–57.

### 60. [David Andrew's Grave]

This grave of David Andrew (right), on Pennock Island near Ketchikan, borrows from Native and white influences. A headstone with English engraving marks the grave, but a memorial pole also honors the person buried here. The marker reads, "Chief's Son David Andrew. Born December 30, 1871. Drowned in Tongass Narrows, March 15, 1903." 87–148

384    Indian totems and graves, Howkan, Alaska.    Copyright 1897 by Winter & Pond.

## 61.  "Indian Totems and Graves, Howkan, Alaska"

This view of the graveyard at Howkan was copyrighted in 1897. It shows
a combination of old and new styles of graves. The killer whale and bear
sculptures, and the small pole, are traditional memorials, but also
present is a grave house decorated with commercially manufactured
turned wood. 87–058

382   Indian totems and graves, Howkan, Alaska.                    Copyright 1897 by Winter & Pond.

## 62. "Indian Totems and Graves, Howkan, Alaska"

The killer whale in the facing photograph (no. 61) is seen in much better
detail in this image. The whale's extremely long dorsal fin is in the
collection of the Burke Museum at the University of Washington, and a
replica of the entire sculpture, carved by artist Bill Holm, was dedicated
there in 1986. 87–057

### 63. "Images on Doctor's Graves, Chilkat"

Winter and Pond reported in *The Totems of Alaska* that these images, near the Tlingit village of Klukwan, marked the grave of Shah, the "most renowned" of the Tlingit ixts. They wrote: "Knee deep in the forest leaves stands Gow-ge-a-deh ("the man with the drum") with arm outstretched. The image, called the servant of Shah, once held an immense drum, which was beaten continuously during the ceremonies attending the healing of the sick." Beside Gow-ge-a-deh is a smaller, upright image standing on a frog. According to Winter and Pond, Shah was a member of the Frog clan. 87–029

# Potlatches and Ceremonial Art

## 64. "Potlatch Dance on Chilkat River, Alaska"

Canoes land on the banks of the Chilkat River, bringing dancers to a potlatch. American
flags were sometimes displayed on these occasions as part of the ceremonial regalia.
Guests were invited from surrounding villages, and invitations were sometimes issued
a year in advance. The photograph was copyrighted in 1895. 87–043

### 65. [Exterior of a Chief's House.] "Chilkat Indians in Old Dancing Costumes, Alaska"

Indians at Klukwan pose in dance regalia. The man in the center, wearing the Chilkat tunic, is Yeilgooxu, the hereditary head of the Klukwan Whale House who appears in photograph 10.* Several of the masks and hats here are pictured in interior views of the Whale House, as are some of the same individuals (nos. 72, 73). One of the men on the right wears a vest and a watch chain along with leather painted bird wings and a decorated spruce root hat. Another man wears a ceremonial mask along with a shirt and necktie. The boy on the left wears the woven hat cover belonging to the tall hat on the far right. The occasion called for dressy clothes, whether from the Native or the Euro-American culture. The dancers combined items from each culture, and Winter and Pond marketed the photograph without trying to remove the signs of white contact. 87–007

* For more detailed information on Yeilgooxu, and on his son Louis Shotridge, see Maureen Milburn, "Louis Shotridge and the Objects of Everlasting Esteem," pp. 54–77.

## 66. "Indian Dancers at Potlatch, Chilkat"

These dancers interrupt their indoors activities to pose for Winter and Pond during a potlatch in Klukwan in late 1894 or 1895. The people in the foreground strike dramatic stances. Some hold masks up for the camera, while others wave eagle feathers. Since they had to stay still in these positions for the length of the exposure, the poses are very deliberate. The photograph shows how people were dressing for potlatches in this time period—a mixture of European clothing and Native tunics and beadwork. The figures in the background with their backs to the camera appear to be dancing. The building they stand before is the Frog House, a two-story community house. According to a Native consultant, the ground floor was used for potlatches, while guests stayed on the upper floor. The dancer on the far right wears a tunic with a frog crest similar to that on the grave house in photograph 58. 87–020

## 67. [Dancers at Klukwan]

Some of the Klukwan dancers pose for a formal portrait. The almost symmetrical arrangement of figures and dance costumes shows that the photographers' concern for composition extended outside the studio. Some of these same people appear in the facing photograph (no. 66), but here they do not strike dramatic action poses. One boy wears a wig and a headdress of mountain goat horn normally reserved for the ixt, or spiritual leader. All of the adults wear nose rings, which were reported to be traditionally worn on both ceremonial and everyday occasions. This practice, which involved piercing the septum of young boys or infants, seems to have been on the decline by 1880.* The boys in this image do not wear them. 87–035

* Krause, *The Tlingit Indians*, pp. 94–95.

196     Indian Dancers, Chilkat, Alaska.     Copyright 1895 by Winter & Pond.

## 68. "Indian Dancers, Chilkat, Alaska"

Three dancers (left) pose in a makeshift tent studio, probably in Klukwan. They wear tunics and leggings of wool and leather ornamented with beadwork. All three have painted faces and nose rings. Painted patterns on faces were part of dance costumes, contributing to the story being enacted. Native consultants report that the colors used were black (from charcoal) and red (from hemlock bark). George von Langsdorff, a German scholar who visited Sitka in 1805, described and sketched Tlingit Indians who danced during trading sessions holding the tail or wing of an eagle, with down feathers from sea eagles on their heads.* Some ninety years later, these dancers display feathers in similar ways. The photograph was copyrighted in 1895. 87–036

* Vaughan and Holm, *Soft Gold*, pp. 234–35. A sketch by von Langsdorff is in The Bancroft Library, University of California, Berkeley. For additional information on von Langsdorff's report, see Erna Gunther, *Indian Life on the Northwest Coast of North America as Seen by the Early Explorers and Fur Traders during the Last Decades of the Eighteenth Century* (Chicago: University of Chicago Press, 1972), pp.175–81.

## 69. "Indian Dancers, Chilkat, Alaska"

With painted faces, dancers stand against the same background seen in the facing photograph (no. 68). Like people in several of the photographs above, they pose with a gun, an item often seen in photographs of dance regalia and other treasured possessions. The men also display a long beaded pouch or wall pocket. The slits open to allow storage, and were reportedly sometimes used to hold papers and letters. One man wears a head-dress made from a fuchsia-colored feather duster, a prized addition to dance costumes. 87–037

Indian Dancers, Chilkat, Alaska.    Winter & Pond, Photo.

Copyright 1895 by Winter & Pond.

## 70. "Chilkat Indian Potlatch Dancers"

Chilkat Indians pose in wool and leather dance tunics ornamented with beadwork. Many wear their dance costumes over Euro-American clothes. One man on the right, posing with a skin drum and beater, has a watch and chain. The dancers belong to various clans, and, according to report, normally would have danced together only at weddings, but they assemble here to pose for the photographer. The longhouse has had commercial trim added to its roof line for ornamentation. The photograph was copyrighted in 1895. 87–023

Exterior of Chief Klart-Reech's House, Chilkat, Alaska.

200

Copyright 1895 by Winter & Pond.

## 71. "Exterior of Chief Klart-Reech's House, Chilkat, Alaska"

These children pose in front of the longhouse, known as the Whale House, of the Gaanaxteidi clan in
Klukwan. Yeilgooxu, or Shotridge (Klart-Reech), the leader of the clan (see also no. 10), was the caretaker
of the house and the art it contained. This picture shows the great size of the communal house and of
the massive spruce timbers used to build it. In the old style, planks are set vertically.* The interior of the
house is shown in photographs 72 and 73. This photograph was copyrighted in 1895. 87–009

* The Whale House is described in detail in Emmons, "The Whale House of the Chilkat," pp. 1–33.

117

## 72. [Interior of the Whale House]

The Whale House in Klukwan contained some of the finest examples of art from the Northwest Coast, including this spectacular house screen, known as the Rain Screen, and several skillfully carved house posts.* Two carved and painted bentwood boxes, spruce root hats, painted leather tunics and "bird wings," a well-worn woven Chilkat dance apron, wooden helmets, and a mask have all been arranged somewhat symmetrically for the photograph. A tall spear is on display, as are two guns. The photographers may have used an extended time exposure, probably supplementing with flash powder the natural light from cracks in the ceiling. 87–013

* Steve Brown discusses the carved house posts in "From Taquan to Klukwan."

### 73. "Interior of Chief Klart-Reech's House, Chilkat, Alaska. Indians in Old Dancing Costumes"

Inside the Whale House, twelve people pose with the objects displayed in photograph 72 and other images above. The spaciousness of the interior of the house conveys its immense size. The man in the center, wearing a leather painted tunic, is probably Coudahwot (see no. 10). Even in this setting, Winter and Pond attended to the conventions of portraiture. Coudahwot's hand rests lightly on the shoulders of the boy in front of him, while the man on the left in the Chilkat dance apron lays his hand on the head of the woodworm feast dish. The giant basket in the foreground (33 inches diameter) was known as the "Mother-Basket." A prized possession of the Gaanaxteidi clan, it was used to serve food to guests on ceremonial occasions.* 87–010

* Milburn, "Louis Shotridge," p. 60; The Chilkat dance apron appears in at least two other photographs (nos. 73 and 86). Frances Paul, *Spruce Root Basketry of the Alaska Tlingit* (1944), describes the "Mother-Basket," pp. 69–71.

## 74. [Ceremonial Art, Klukwan]

Many of the same art objects being worn in the other Klukwan photographs appear here. They are displayed around a house post that bears the image of a ceremonial copper, an object that played important roles in ceremonies. The "Mother-Basket" hangs by the flag. The Chilkat dancing blankets were woven from mountain goat wool and cedar bark by female artists who copied designs on pattern boards painted by male artists. The pattern boards provided only slightly more than one half the design, so the weavers had to create a mirror image to produce a symmetrical blanket. The blanket on the righthand side of the photograph was probably made from the pattern board leaning vertically behind it. The blanket on the far left has a very similar design. 87–161

## 75. [Man with Ceremonial Art, Klukwan]

Here a man models the Chilkat dancing apron and one of the dancing blankets.* The blanket on the right hangs over a camphorwood chest from China. Fur traders introduced these chests during the maritime fur trade that lasted from the late eighteenth to the early nineteenth centuries. Among the Indians, they became prized storage containers for ceremonial regalia. They were sometimes displayed along with the elaborately carved and painted ceremonial chests made by Native artists.† The American flag stands to the left of the house post. Its presence in this photograph suggests that its Native owner may have considered it part of his ceremonial regalia. 87–230

* The painted leather wing hanging from his neck was more typically displayed as seen in photograph 65.

† Vaughan and Holm, *Soft Gold*, p. 20.

202 OLD TOTEM POLES IN CHIEF'S HOUSE CHILKAT
COPYRIGHT BY WINTER & POND.

## 76. "Old Totem Poles in Chief's House, Chilkat"

A young girl poses inside the Frog House of the Gaanaxteidi clan of Klukwan, in front of a wooden house post. She wears a button blanket of wool trimmed with pearl buttons, and sits neatly on a wood sculpture of a head, which was moved there to serve as her seat. The sculpture to the left originally stood at the inner entrance of the house. It was sketched by German geographer Aurel Krause, who studied the Tlingit in Klukwan in 1881.* 87–017

* Krause, *The Tlingit Indians*, p. 89.

## 77. [Indians in Ceremonial Dress, Klinquan]

Winter and Pond marketed the image at right under the name "Chilkat Dancers," but it was actually taken around 1900 in Klinquan, a Haida village on Prince of Wales Island far to the south of the Tlingit Chilkat region, and the people in the picture are Haida Indians. The marchers have been identified, from left, as Donald Mekatla or Robert Edenshaw; unknown man; Kasawak (Edwin Scott); unknown man; Eddie or Hugh Cogo; Ankileq (Mike George); and Nasauk. The two figures in the foreground are Matthew Collison and Gennowwu (Ben Duncan).* 87–316

* Identifications, and the current locations of the art pieces in the photographs, are discussed in more detail by Ronald Weber in "Photographs as Ethnographic Documents," pp. 67–78. The documentation is derived from interviews with Mrs. Helen Sanderson conducted by Margaret B. Blackman in 1971, and from interviews with M. (or Emma) Lawrence in 1975 and Robert and Nora Cogo in 1977.

Winter & Pond Photo.

### 78. "Takou Chief Lying in State, Alaska"

A high-ranking Tlingit leader lies in state indoors, surrounded by art objects and other prized possessions. His ceremonial art on display includes two Chilkat woven tunics, a tunic with a bear crest outlined in dentalium shells, a crest helmet, and a frontlet with a long train of white ermine furs. The body is covered with a button blanket, and a fur helmet crowns the head. Guns and a felt hat are displayed prominently. A patchwork quilt is spread in a corner. A clock, a small pitcher, and a rocking chair show some of the appurtenances of daily living in the house. Winter and Pond circulated this picture commercially, cropping it where they have added the tape to the negative. 87–268

## 79. [Man Lying in State]

A Tlingit leader (the same man who stood for his portrait in photograph 15) lies in state on a wooden bed, wearing his ceremonial frontlet of wood, abalone shell, sea lion whiskers, flicker feathers, and ermine skin. A ceremonial clan hat rests on his body. He is covered with a wool blanket decorated with appliqué and buttons, to which a wool beaded pouch has been attached. A wool trade blanket is visible under the button blanket, while an elaborate Chilkat dancing blanket is displayed above the body. In the background, a large poster advertises that a photographer will be in the Northwest in June and advises clients to "avoid the rush." This appears to be the poster of one of the several photographers who traveled to Alaska in the summers. It may have been used to patch the wall. In one release of this photograph, Winter and Pond labeled the man a Takou chief; in another release, they called him a Chilkat chief. The former designation is probably accurate, for the crest hat has been documented as belonging to the Gaanaxteidi Taku family.* 87–267

* Holm, *The Box of Daylight* (Seattle: Seattle Art Museum and University of Washington Press, 1983), p. 43; and Holm, pers. comm., June 1988.

## 80.  [Infant Lying in State]

High-ranking babies also had a lying-in-state period
during mourning ceremonies. This child is covered
with white ermine skins. The body is surrounded by
three Chilkat blankets and by beaded work. 87–262

## 81. [Chilkat Dancing Blanket]

Chilkat ceremonial dancing blankets were woven from mountain goat hair mixed with cedar bark, using complex, sophisticated weaving techniques that enabled the weavers to produce curved lines and circles. The designs on the blankets represented crest figures, but they are so abstract that interpretations about their identity often differ. According to George Emmons, the design on this blanket represents a killer whale. The inverted face in the center depicts the whale's body; the whale's head is split and appears in two profiles on the bottom half of the blanket.* While Winter and Pond photographed Chilkat blankets being worn and displayed in traditional contexts, here they hung the blanket on the side of a building to photograph it.  87–159

* Emmons, *The Chilkat Blanket*, p. 387; Bill Holm, pers. comm., June 1988.

## 82. "Native Women Weaving Baskets, Sitka, Alaska"

In Sitka in 1897, Tlingit basket weavers pose for Winter and Pond with unfinished spruce root baskets (right). In the foreground in the center is a bundle of grass used to make designs in a weaving technique known as false embroidery. A few finished "curios" are displayed for the camera, including pouches decorated with tiny beads, and a glass flask covered with basketry. The woman in the center wears two silver bracelets engraved with Native designs. Weaving baskets for the tourist market became an important source of income for Native women, who had fewer wage-earning opportunities in white industries than did males. 87–106

### 83. "Basket Weaver, Howkan, Alaska"

Winter and Pond arranged several completed baskets and a mat around this weaver from the Haida village of Howkan. She is splitting cedar bark to create fibers the right width for weaving. Gripping one end of the bark strip in her teeth, she separates the strands by applying pressure with her hands. She wears silver rings on every finger, at least some of which are of Native craftsmanship. 87–064

## 84. [Weaving a Chilkat Dancing Blanket]

Here a weaver works on a Chilkat ceremonial dancing blanket. She has completed the border on three sides and is starting to weave the design elements in the center of the blanket. The long strands of the warp are bundled to keep them clean and tangle-free. Newspapers have been placed over both ends of the blanket to protect the finished border. They are dated January 12, 1904, and apparently originated in California. The weaver wears many items of jewelry, some made by Indians and some probably purchased from Caucasians.*  87–197

* Additional information on the weaving of Chilkat blankets can be found in Samuel, *The Chilkat Dancing Blanket*.

Indian Totem Pole Carver at Work, Fort Wrangel, Alaska.    Winter & Pond, Photo.

## 85. "Indian Totem Pole Carver at Work, Fort Wrangel, Alaska"

A Tlingit man carves a human figure. This image, the only known Winter and Pond view of a carver at work, appears to be posed. The man wears a ceremonial tunic decorated with buttons, and a cap made from a bear's head. While a carver occasionally would wear a ceremonial blanket while carving, this man's headdress was probably donned for the camera. The man holds the knife in traditional fashion, with his thumb pointing toward the handle rather than toward the blade. 87–257

## 86. [Chilkat Dance Apron]

Winter and Pond photographed this dance apron being worn in Klukwan in 1895 (see nos. 73, 75). Like the larger Chilkat ceremonial blankets, it is woven of mountain goat hair and cedar bark using a complex technique. The design represents a beaver, identified by prominent incisors and the cross-hatched tail. Puffin beaks hang from the leather fringe, creating a rustling sound when the dancer moved. According to oral tradition, this apron may have been the first Chilkat blanket that came to Klukwan. 87–157

Mr & Mrs. John T. Spickett's display of Alaska Baskets.

Winter&Pond
Juneau

### 87. "Mr. & Mrs. John T. Spickett's display of Alaska Baskets"

Basket collecting was a favorite hobby of many whites, and large groups of baskets
made impressive displays. Here, the Spicketts, residents of Juneau, stand with 122
baskets showing a variety of designs. 87–177

## 88. [Carved House Post]

At an old village site along the coast, a carved house post supports the frame of a communal house long since abandoned. With the adze-hewn massive side beams of the house resting behind its ears, it stands as silent testimony to a way of life still honored in memory. 87–1350

# *Appendix A.* Note on Methodology

My goal in the preceding discussion has been to present a wide range of the Winter and Pond images of Indians from southeast Alaska, emphasizing the ways in which the photographs serve as an historical illustration of people responding to changes prompted by foreign settlement. Often ethnohistorical photographs are analyzed principally to assess their ethnographic accuracy. The objective here was somewhat different: to trace what the photographs reflect about resiliency and adaptation in the face of rapid change, and to explore what they may indicate about attitudes toward art, Native-white relations, and other topics that rest beneath the surface of the photograph.

A range of sources, both human and archival, contributed to the research. Unfortunately, with the exception of a few short commercial publications and a few notations about printing that the photographers left on negative sleeves, there is little known written material by Winter and Pond. No diaries or journals have been found that shed light on their motivations. It is necessary to rely almost entirely on the images themselves to suggest conclusions.

Biographical information on Winter and Pond has previously been made available in Wendy Calmensen's master's thesis and in the article by Robert De Armond based on that work. In order to include the greatest number of photographs possible, the preceding discussion mentions primarily the data that relate directly to Winter and Pond's activities photographing Indians.

As active members of the Juneau community, Winter and Pond received loyal coverage in local newspapers. Articles—or short notes in "items of local interest" columns—occasionally refer to notable activities such as their trips, their promotion of tourist "excursions," their participation in community organizations, and their work collecting exhibits for the Alaska-Yukon-Pacific Exposition. Their newspaper advertisements help document the services they offered and the clientele they hoped to attract. Some newspapers and magazines published Winter and Pond images as illustrations with their stories.

Contemporary consultants, both Native and Caucasian, were very helpful in providing information about activities and customs portrayed in the photographs.* Native consultants were sought who come from and are familiar with the villages shown in the images. Studying each image, they gave valuable insights about the people, art pieces, houses, and activities depicted in the photographs. They noted changes documented in the photographs, and also commented on changes that have taken place since the images were taken. All their comments helped determine important images to display.

Portraits were generally taken too long ago to allow positive identification of their subjects today, and identifying the locations of specific houses in some village scenes proved similarly problematic. Unfortunately, as has been noted, Winter and Pond did not often record proper names and were occasionally inconsistent in labeling images. Thus, some geographical attributions are suspect.

Inexplicably, a few negatives of images attributed to other photographers are now part of the Winter and Pond Collection. These include photographs perhaps taken by William H. Case and Herbert Draper in Juneau, and several made by Fhoki Kayamori in Yakutat. Such images have not been included in this discussion as it is not clear whether the negatives were acquired—or copied—personally by Winter and Pond or became mixed in with the Winter and Pond negatives after their deaths.

Considering the number of images Winter and Pond took, it is surprising how few copies exist in repositories today. Large North American archives of ethnohistorical photographs frequently have a few images, but none in significant quantities. While it is possible that Winter and Pond made few copies of each image, it is more likely that material of this nature—unlike "curios"—has not typically made its way into repositories. This makes the glass plate and nitrate negative collection at the Alaska State Library all the more valuable, for it is useful to analyze the images together as a body of work by a team of photographers.

Much promising research remains to be done on the Winter and Pond collection of Native images. Detailed analysis may be made of the ethnographic information in each image. Such an effort, correlating the images with extensive and specific information from ethnographies and oral informants, would prove rewarding. Similarly, many of the totem poles and ceremonial art pieces pictured in the Winter and Pond photographs exist today, on location or in museums. It would be fruitful to trace their history and use from the time the photographs were taken to the present, and to unite copies of the images with the original art pieces.

Extensive comparisons of Winter and Pond's work with that of other contemporaneous photographers of Alaskan Indians would provide more basis for speculation about the changes and the attitudes the images reflect. The preceding discussion has implicitly asserted that there is no "representative" portrait of a southeast Alaskan Indian from the late nineteenth century. The study of further images showing related subjects would provide more data about the range of experiences. An examination of images from many Alaskan photographers would be extremely productive, and suggests similar "regional studies" of photographs from other areas of the American West. Such a massive undertaking is made more feasible with the introduction of microfiche. Hundreds of images from the University of Washington, the Alaska State Library, and the Polar Archives at the Rasmuson Library, University of Fairbanks, are now available in this form.

Such a study would certainly include extensive oral history and consultation with Tlingit and Haida Indians in villages throughout southeast Alaska. The Winter and Pond photographs, and other collections from their era, provide a promising basis for recording very specific information such as Tlingit and Haida names for individual places, buildings, and activities seen in the images. Some people can relate stories in the oral tradition about events that took place during the era of the photographs. Others can discuss changes that occurred in the decades after the photographs were taken. The preceding discussion, which is directed toward a geographically broad, general audience, has not presented such specific data about each image in detail. However, research with oral consultants made it clear how fruitful such a detailed and comprehensive study would be, and how important it is to preserve the information and insights of the descendants of the people who posed in the photographs.

* Native consultants remain anonymous here in keeping with options in the National Endowment for the Humanities regulations.

# *Appendix B.* Index to photographs

*PCA refers to the catalogue number at the Alaska State Library.*

**PCA       TITLE**

*A killer whale sculpture stands among memorial poles in the graveyard at the Haida village of Howkan, c. 1897.*

# References

BOOKS

Barbeau, Marius. 1950. *Totem Poles*. National Museum of Canada, Bulletin 119, Anthropological Series 30. 2 vols. Ottawa: National Museums of Canada.

Blackman, Margaret B. 1981. *Window on the Past: The Photographic Ethnohistory of the Northern and Kaigani Haida*. Canadian Ethnology Service Paper No. 74. Ottawa: National Museums of Canada.

Cole, Douglas. 1985. *Captured Heritage: The Scamble for Northwest Coast Artifacts*. Seattle: University of Washington Press; Vancouver, B.C.: Douglas and McIntyre.

Crawford, William. 1979. *The Keepers of Light: A History and Working Guide to Early Photographic Processes*. Dobbs Ferry, N.Y.: Morgan and Morgan.

De Armond, Robert N., ed. 1981. *Lady Franklin Visits Sitka, Alaska, 1870: The Journal of Sophia Cracroft, Sir John Franklin's Niece*. Anchorage: Alaska Historical Society.

Edelstein, Susan F., ed. 1980. *Carved History: The Totem Poles and House Posts of Sitka National Historical Park*. Anchorage: Alaska Natural History Association.

Emmons, George. 1907. *The Chilkat Blanket*. With notes on the blanket designs by Franz Boas. American Museum of Natural History Memoir No. 3, pt. 4, pp. 329–401. New York: American Museum of Natural History.

Fleming, Paula R., and Judith Luskey. 1986. *The North American Indians in Early Photographs*. New York: Harper and Row.

Gunther, Erna. 1972. *Indian Life on the Northwest Coast of North America As Seen by the Early Explorers and Fur Traders During the Last Decades of the Eighteenth Century*. Chicago: University of Chicago Press.

Halpin, Marjorie M. 1981. *Totem Poles: An Illustrated Guide*. Vancouver: University of British Columbia Press.

Higginson, Ella. 1908. *Alaska: The Great Country*. New York: Macmillan Company.

Hinckley, Ted C. 1982. *Alaskan John G. Brady: Missionary, Businessman, Judge, and Governor, 1878–1918*. Published for Miami University by Ohio State University Press.

Holm, Bill. 1983. *The Box of Daylight: Northwest Coast Indian Art*. Seattle: Seattle Art Museum and University of Washington Press.

Holm, Bill, and Bill Reid. 1975. *Form and Freedom: A Dialogue on Northwest Coast Indian Art*. Houston: Institute for the Arts, Rice University. (Reprinted as *Indian Art of the Northwest Coast: A Dialogue on Craftsmanship and Aesthetics*, Seattle: University of Washington Press, 1976).

Holmberg, Heinrich Johan. 1985. *Holmberg's Ethnographic Sketches*. Edited by Marvin W. Falk. Fairbanks: University of Alaska Press. (Originally published 1855–63).

Jonaitis, Aldona. 1986. *Art of the Northern Tlingit*. Seattle: University of Washington Press.

Kamenskii, Fr. Anatolii. 1985. *Tlingit Indians of Alaska*. Fairbanks: University of Alaska Press. (Originally published in Odessa, 1906).

Kaplan, Susan A., and Kristin J. Barsness. 1986. *Raven's Journey: The World of Alaska's Native People*. Philadelphia: The University Museum, University of Pennsylvania.

Keithahn, Edward L. 1963. *Monuments in Cedar: The Authentic Story of the Totem Pole*. Second edition. New York: Bonanza Books.

Krause, Aurel. 1956. *The Tlingit Indians: Results of a Trip to the Northwest Coast of America and the Bering Straits*. Translated by Erna Gunther. Seattle: University of Washington Press. (Originally published in German in 1885.)

de Laguna, Frederica. 1960. *The Story of a Tlingit Community: A Problem in the Relationship Between Archaeological, Ethnological and Historical Methods*. Washington, D.C.: U.S. Government Printing Office.

de Laguna, Frederica. 1972. *Under Mount Saint Elias: The History and Culture of the Yakutat Tlingit*. Smithsonian Contributions to Anthropology, vol. 7 (in three parts).

La Violette, Forrest E. 1961. *The Struggle For Survival: Indian Cultures and the Protestant Ethic in British Columbia*. Toronto: University of Toronto Press.

Lyman, Christopher M. 1982. *The Vanishing Race and Other Illusions: Photographs of Indians by Edward S. Curtis*. Washington, D.C.: Smithsonian Institution Press.

McClintock, Eva, ed. 1884. *Life in Alaska: Letters of Mrs. Eugene S. Willard*. Philadelphia: Presbyterian Board of Education.

Macnair, Peter, Alan Hoover, and Kevin Neary. 1984. *The Legacy: Tradition and Innovation in Northwest Coast Indian Art*. Vancouver: Douglas and McIntyre; Seattle: University of Washington Press.

Niblack, Albert P. 1970. *The Coast Indians of Southern Alaska and Northern British Columbia*. H. Mis. 142, pt. 2–15. New York: Johnson Reprint Corp.

Paul, Frances. 1944. *Spruce Root Basketry of the Alaska Tlingit*.

Sackett, Russell. 1979. *The Chilkat Tlingit: A General Overview*. Anthropology and Historic Preservation Cooperative Park Studies Unit, University of Alaska, Occasional Paper No. 23.

Samuel, Cheryl. 1982. *The Chilkat Dancing Blanket*. Seattle: Pacific Search Press.

Sewid-Smith, Daisy (My-yah-nelth). 1979. *Prosecution or Persecution*. British Columbia: Nu-Yum-Baleess Society.

Steltzer, Ulli. 1984. *A Haida Potlatch*. Vancouver: Douglas and McIntyre; Seattle: University of Washington Press.

Taft, Robert. 1964. *Photography and the American Scene*. New York: Dover Publications. (Originally published in 1938.)

Vaughan, Thomas, and Bill Holm. 1982. *Soft Gold: The Fur Trade and Cultural Exchange on the Northwest Coast of America*. Portland: Oregon Historical Society.

Winter, Lloyd, and Percy Pond. 1905. *The Totems of Alaska.* New York: The Albertype Company.

Wright, Julia McN. 1893. *Among the Alaskans.* Philadelphia: Presbyterian Board of Home Missions.

Wyatt, Victoria. 1984. *Shapes of Their Thoughts: Reflections of Culture Contact in Northwest Coast Indian Art.* New Haven: Yale Peabody Museum and University of Oklahoma Press.

Young, S. Hall. 1927. *Hall Young of Alaska, "The Mushing Parson": The Autobiography of S. Hall Young.* New York and Chicago: Fleming H. Revell Co.


ARTICLES

Blackman, Margaret B. 1976. "Creativity in Acculturation: Art, Architecture and Ceremony from the Northwest Coast," *Ethnohistory* 23(4):387–413.

Blackman, Margaret B. 1981–82. " 'Copying People': Northwest Coast Native Responses to Early Photography," *B.C. Studies* 52:86–108.

Brown, Steve. 1987. "From Taquan to Klukwan: Tracing the Work of an Early Tlingit Master Artist," in Peter L. Corey, ed. *Faces, Voices and Dreams: A Celebration of the Centennial of the Sheldon Jackson Museum,* pp. 157–75. Sitka, Alaska: Alaska State Dept. of Education and Friends of the Sheldon Jackson Museum.

Carpenter, Edmund. 1976. "Introduction," in Bill Holm and Bill Reid, *Indian Art of the Northwest Coast: A Dialogue on Craftsmanship and Aesthetics.* Seattle: University of Washington Press. (Originally published 1975 under the title *Form and Freedom: A Dialogue on Northwest Coast Indian Art.*)

De Armond, Robert N. 1982. "Winter and Pond, Photographers, 1893–1956," *Alaska Journal,* Winter: 10–20.

De Armond, Robert N. 1987. "The History of the Sheldon Jackson Museum," in Peter L. Corey, ed. *Faces, Voices and Dreams: A Celebration of the Centennial of the Sheldon Jackson Museum,* pp. 3–19. Sitka, Alaska: Alaska State Dept. of Education, and Friends of the Sheldon Jackson Museum.

Emmons, George T. 1916. "The Whale House of the Chilkat," *Anthropological Papers of the American Museum of Natural History* 19(1):1–33.

Hinckley, Ted C. 1964 "Sheldon Jackson as Preserver of Alaska's Native Culture," *Pacific Historical Review* 33:411–24.

Holm, Bill. 1983. "The Vanishing Race and Other Illusions," *American Indian Art Magazine* 8(3):68–73.

Holm, Bill. 1985. "Old Photos Might Not Lie, But They Fib a Lot about Color!" *American Indian Art Magazine* 10(4):44–49.

Kan, Sergei. 1987. "Memory Eternal: Orthodox Christianity and the Tlingit Mortuary Complex," *Arctic Anthropology* 24(1):32–55.

Keithahn, E. L. 1981. "The Authentic History of Shakes Island and Clan." Wrangell: Wrangell Historical Society; reprinted from a pamphlet printed by the Wrangell *Sentinel,* 1940.

Milburn, Maureen. 1986. "Louis Shotridge and the Objects of Everlasting Esteem," in Kaplan and Barsness, *Raven's Journey: The World of Alaska's Native People,* pp. 54–77. Philadelphia: The University Museum, University of Pennsylvania.

Pierce, Richard A. 1975. "Voznesenskii—Scientist in Alaska," *Alaska Journal* 4(1):11–15.

Roppel, Patricia. 1975. "Loring," *Alaska Journal* 5(3):169–78.

Scherer, Joanna. 1975. "Pictures as Documents: Resources for the Study of North American Ethnohistory," and "You Can't Believe Your Eyes: Inaccuracies in Photographs of North American Indians," *Studies in the Anthropology of Visual Communications* 2(2):65–79.

Seward, Frederick W. 1973. "Eclipse at Chilkat," *Alaska Journal* 2(1):18–20.

Sherman, Ro, ed. 1974. "The Village of Klukwan, by E. J. Glave of the Frank Leslie's Illustrated Newspaper Expedition to Alaska," *Alaska Journal* 4(2):82–87.

Weber, Ronald L. 1985. "Photographs as Ethnographic Documents," *Arctic Anthropology* 22(1):67–78.

Whipkey, Reverend A. J. 1909. "Last Winter at Hoonah," *Assembly Herald* 15(6):269–70.

Wyatt, Victoria. 1986 "A Unique Attraction: The Alaskan Totem Poles at St. Louis Exposition of 1904," in Terrence Cole, ed., *The Alaska Journal: A 1986 Collection,* pp. 14–23. Anchorage: Alaska Northwest Publishing Company.

Wyatt, Victoria. 1987. "Alaskan Indian Wage Earners in the 19th Century: Economic Choices and Ethnic Identity on Southeast Alaska's Frontier," *Pacific Northwest Quarterly* 78(1–2):43–49.


REPORTS

Emmons, G. T. 1905. "A Report on the Conditions and Needs of the Natives of Alaska." 58th Cong., 3d Sess., Sen. Ex. Doc. 106, p. 2, Serial 4765.

Glass, Henry. 1881. Letters of Commander Henry Glass to Secretary of the Navy (March and June), "Commanders' Letters 1881 Navy Department." National Archives, Code M 147, Roll 116.

Lopp, William T. 1910. "Report on the Education of the Natives of Alaska and the Reindeer Service." Reprint of chapter 33, Bureau of Education, Report of the Commissioner for 1910, with an appendix, p. xv (Washington, D.C.: U.S. Government Printing Office). (Also in 61st Cong., 3d Sess., H.R. Doc. 1006, Ser. 5978.)

Swanton, John R. 1908. "Social Conditions, Beliefs, and Linguistic Relationship of the Tlingit Indians." *Twenty-sixth Annual Report of the Bureau of American Ethnology,* pp. 391–486. Washington, D.C.

Swineford, Alfred P. 1887. "Report of the Governor of Alaska to the Secretary of the Interior, 1887." Washington, D.C.: U.S. Government Printing Office.

## MANUSCRIPTS

Alaska State Library finder's aid to Winter and Pond PCA 87.

Governor John Green Brady Papers, Beinecke Rare Book and Manuscript Library, Yale University, New Haven.

Calmensen, Wendy. 1979. "Winter and Pond: Pioneer Photographers in Alaska, 1893–1943." Master's thesis, San Francisco State University.

Hinckley, Ted C. 1987. "A New Perspective on the Navy's Destruction of the Tlingit Indian Village of Angoon in 1882." Paper delivered at the Eighth Naval History Symposium, U.S. Naval Academy, September 25.

Kan, Sergei. 1982. " 'Wrap Your Father's Brothers in Kind Words': An Analysis of the Nineteenth-Century Tlingit Mortuary and Memorial Rituals." Ph.D. dissertation, University of Chicago.

## NEWSPAPERS

*Alaska Daily Empire*
*Alaskan*
*Alaska News*
*Alaska Record Miner*
*Alaska Searchlight*
*Daily Alaska Dispatch*
*Daily Alaska Empire*
*Juneau Independent*

# Text Index

## ABOUT THE AUTHOR

Victoria Wyatt is assistant professor of art history, and curator of Northwest Coast Indian art for the Thomas Burke Memorial Washington State Museum, University of Washington. An ethnohistorian specializing in the history of Native-white relations on the Northwest Coast and in Alaska, she has worked extensively with nonwritten sources.